About the Author

Rob has co-written two full-length musicals and written two plays, all of which have been staged. Rob wrote a book about his English Channel swim in 2012 called *From Starr to Starrfish*, which was published in 2013. Rob lives in Brighton with his wife Sharon and their three children, Asher, Mia and Jesse. Rob's passion is open water swimming and he swims every morning at 6:30am throughout the year from the Palace Pier in Brighton. This is Rob's first novel.

ROB STARR

WHAT THE TIDE BRINGS BACK

JUST ONCE

PUBLISHING

First published in 2024 by Just Once Publishing Ltd
Copyright © Rob Starr 2024

Rob Starr has asserted his right to be identified as the author of this Work in accordance with the Copyright, Designs and Patents Act 1988.

ISBN: 978-1-7394101-0-0

Editing and design by Fuzzy Flamingo
www.fuzzyflamingo.co.uk

A catalogue for this book is available from the British Library.

Before meeting Marlene Woolgar, I am not sure if I truly believed in the spirit world. Now I am a believer – she is the best.

All my friends at Brighton Swimming Club who swim with me in the sea at 6.30 each morning throughout the year in all weathers and keep me safe – the best mermaids and mermen I could wish for. A special shout out to Big Bob Bicknell – shoulder to shoulder, always my friend.

And to my wife Sharon and children, Asher, Mia and Jesse for making me laugh even when I don't want to.

Sometimes, what gets washed up with the tide is more than just the bones.

The only reason for time is so that everything doesn't happen at once.

— *Albert Einstein*

CHAPTER ONE

Lilly Baker

1851

As the rest of the workhouse slept, Melody and Lilly eased open the door to his room and slid into the corner.

The room was large by comparison to their dormitory, big enough to fit twenty of them side by side, but it was as sparse and cold as theirs, which surprised them; he had never taken them to his room and they had assumed it would be filled with the fruits of his dishonesty. The single bed was in the far corner and not big enough for his bulky frame, causing his body to loll unnaturally. Apart from the bed, the room contained a small cupboard for his clothes, and a corner dressing table with a single drawer in the centre. His perfume bottle was lying in the middle, the burnt orange scent creeping from it and itching at their throats as it always did when he was near.

Melody and Lilly looked at each other and instinctively knew that the drawer contained keys to the front door. The light in the room came from half a dozen small slits in the top of the outside wall, allowing shards of light through, but not giving the outside world any clue as to what lay within. The moonlight bathed the room in an ethereal glow, making Lilly feel as if she were crawling deeper and deeper into one of the old cellars underneath the streets of London. Sister Spires had spoken about them with passion at the last teaching session, painting a picture in their minds of floating souls lost in the catacombs under their feet for hundreds of years. Father Stevens insisted upon history lessons of London for all the girls. He would make sure that they were educated by the time they left the workhouse. The traders – his greatest source of income – needed the girls they took to be able to hold a conversation if the occasion required.

Watching him lying in bed, Lilly discovered that even when he was fast asleep, his face still showed the same discomfort he portrayed when he was marching through the hallways of the house. It struck her that perhaps the pain and humiliation he doled out to them on a daily basis was nothing more than a reflection of the torment he felt inside. She hated him more in that moment than she ever had before. She walked over to his bed, slipping a wooden-handled kitchen knife from the sleeve of her white nightdress until it sat firmly in her right hand. Without a pause or a look back at Melody, she plunged the knife deep into his throat right up to its handle, her left arm stretching over his fat body to cover his mouth with her free hand, stifling any noise that tried to escape.

His eyes opened wide in shock and fixed on Lilly's; they were the last thing he would ever see.

"Oh my God, Lilly, what have you done?" Melody whispered into the darkness, as she stumbled away from the bed and found herself leaning back against the single cupboard.

Cowering away from Lilly, who was by now covered in Father Stevens' blood, Melody sank to the floor, her knees curling up into a ball to her chest. "It was the only way, Mel," Lilly replied, leaving the knife embedded in Father Stevens' throat as she calmly walked towards the cupboard.

Bathed in the beams of moonlight coming from the window slits, her dress and hands soaked with blood and a soft smile on her face, Lilly looked like a demon conjured from Melody's worst nightmares.

Lilly crouched down beside her and spoke in a whisper. "If

I'd just run away, Mel, he would have known you'd helped me and he would have punished you, wouldn't he? He would have hurt you so bad then sold you off to the traders. I couldn't let that happen. Do you remember when little Sally hid in the laundry room after the lights were out and he thought Kathryn had helped her escape? He beat Kathryn half to death, and even when Sally was eventually found, he sold them both on. I couldn't do that to my big sister, could I? I have to protect my family; we have to look after each other, don't we?"

"We're not sisters, Lilly. You know that, don't you? We're not really sisters."

Lilly didn't move, her smile never wavering, as if everything that was happening was totally reasonable.

"None of us here are really sisters, we were just left here, weren't we? Left on the steps, that's all," Melody continued, trying to keep the madness around her from sending her spiralling into insanity.

She kept her eyes low to avoid looking at Lilly's bloody hands or Father Stevens' lifeless body.

"Of course we're sisters, Melody. We're all sisters, ain't we? We're real family, we are," Lilly said, looking down at her own dress. "Blood don't make family, does it? Not really." She shook her head. "No, it's love that makes family, and we do love each other, don't we, Mel?"

"Lilly…" Melody croaked, the tears starting down her face as she desperately tried not to look up.

"It's all right, Mel, it's all right now," she said, taking Melody's hand in her own, their roles of big sister and little sister now reversed. "Just tell the sisters that you heard something in the night and followed the sound, which drew you here. You saw me running from the room as you came in here and found him. They'll believe you cos you stayed here rather than ran. They'll know you could've run but you didn't. They'll believe you," Lilly repeated, convincing herself she was doing all this just to protect Melody. "Give *me* time to run, though, won't you?" she continued. "And then raise the alarm. I'll be long gone by then."

Melody raised her face and looked deeply into Lilly's eyes. "Where will you go? You can't walk the streets like that."

"I don't know," said Lilly, suddenly confused. "I'm gonna find me a family, ain't I?"

"We don't 'ave family, Lilly. That's why we're here. No one wants us." She said this with a sudden force as the strength came back to her. She pulled herself up to standing so she could once again look down at her roommate and take the role of big sister again. "We ain't got family, you stupid girl."

Without a warning, Lilly grabbed Melody by the throat and shoved her hard into the cupboard door, her small frame throwing the bigger girl backwards as if she were just a bag of feathers. Melody felt a pain sharp in her back as the breath left her body and she again sank back to the floor.

"Lilly…" Melody whispered as all the fight left her.

Lilly's features softened and she crouched down and took the shaking girls hands into her own. "There's a family somewhere waiting for me, Mel, I know there is, I just know it. I'll have a daughter of my own one day, I will. I'll love her too, just like we should be loved. I got to go now. I'll come back for you as soon as I can. I won't leave you here forever, not my big sister." She hugged Melody tightly, the blood smearing both of their clothes. "You'll be fine now without Father Stevens to punish you. No one will suspect you had anything to do with me running away, and the governors will put a new father in, won't they? Maybe they'll even put a new sister in charge, someone who'll do things right by everyone."

Melody nodded, scared to speak.

Lilly walked over to the small vanity unit. She pulled the drawer open, not even trying to hide the noise made by the warped wood as she forced it open. She snatched the keys and then scooped up the bottle of perfume, putting it in her pocket without realising what she was doing. She bent down to give Melody a final kiss goodbye, her hands leaving bloody prints on her sister's cheek as she cupped her face and looked lovingly into her terrified eyes, then she left the room without another sound.

The workhouse was silent and dark as Lilly walked through it, even the rats seemingly afraid to come out and investigate the smell of death that was starting to seep from the room.

Lilly was down the hall and out of the front door in a few seconds. She briefly stood on the top step, bathed in the moonlight, a macabre silhouette. She took the steps slowly, one at a time, her small feet leaving a trail of blood on each one. She crossed the road and headed down the same alleyway where her father had abandoned her fourteen years earlier before he had run off into the night.

★★★

Daisy woke terrified, her body covered in sweat and with a scream trying to escape from her lips. Alfie sensed his twin's distress and woke up at the exact same moment. Scrambling down the ladder from the top bunk, he threw his arms around her before the terror could take hold.

"It's OK, Daisy, I've got you," he whispered into her ear as her breathing started to slow. "Was it her again, the girl in the orphanage?"

"I killed someone, Alfie. I killed him, and there was so much blood; it was everywhere. I can still taste it."

Daisy violently pushed her brother away, scared the blood was still all over her. Alfie saw the fear in her eyes and pulled her back in close to himself once again.

His breath warmed her face as he whispered into her ear, "It wasn't you, Daisy, it was her, Lilly. She did it, not you. She's just showing you, isn't she? You told me that's what she does."

"Yes, it was her, wasn't it? It wasn't me." The relief on her face was hidden in the darkened room. "Stay with me, Alfie," she said as she lay back down and put her head onto her pillow. Alfie said nothing as he snuggled into his sister, both of them drifting back into a deep sleep, all thoughts and dreams of a long-forgotten murder fading away quickly.

CHAPTER TWO

Jesse

2020

A t this time of year, especially on a clear day, the sun rose in the east just above the marina wall, like a ball of fire climbing from the depths of the sea. It was magnificent to witness, a reward for those who forced themselves out of bed early every morning no matter the weather, while others dreamt on, warm and snug.

"Do you have to go so early, Jesse?"

Susie was barely awake when Jesse climbed out of the bed.

"Just stay for another hour," she said as her eyes tried to focus on the clock by the bed showing it was just turning six-thirty in the morning. "You were tossing and turning all night again, you must be shattered," she said, still half asleep.

"I always swim at seven, you know that."

"You can miss it just this once."

She leaned forward on her elbows to watch Jesse pull on his jeans and throw the jumper over his head.

"It's so cold out there, Jesse. Surely, you'd rather stay with me a bit longer."

"Gotta go, Susie, sorry."

Jesse gave her a quick kiss on the forehead before he headed out of the room.

"Will I see you tonight?" she called as she heard the front door open, but there was no reply.

Jesse had already gone.

He headed out of the flat, his swimming bag in hand, and crossed the road to the seafront. He liked Susie, liked her a lot actually, but he was simply not a commitment sort of guy. At first, it had seemed quite handy that he lived in the flat at the top of the house and she lived in the basement flat, with just three floors separating them, it seemed like the perfect set-up. Now, he wondered to himself when it had turned from a bit of fun into a full-blown relationship. He realised that while he had been looking for something just in the moment, she had been planning something for the future. He stopped on the steps and closed his eyes, trying to picture a time when he might settle down with her, or anyone for that matter; but the picture was not an easy one to conjure up.

His DNA did not include the necessary strands that dictated the need for a long-term relationship.

Jesse breathed in, letting his lungs fill with the sea air, and tried to shake off the remnants of the dream that had robbed him of sleep once again – it was the same dream he'd been having for the past year of a little girl covered in blood, and of raging seas and murderous waves; of terror, her terror. It was a nightmare that he had relived every night for months. It was this nightmare that had first led him into the sea off Brighton Beach.

Soon after the dreams had begun, he had felt an incredible draw to be near to the sea, almost a compulsion. And it was this that had led him to join the Brighton Sea Swimming Club. From the first day he had walked into their clubhouse next to the Brighton Palace Pier, the draw to the ocean had become so strong that he had not missed a single morning swim, not one. He had become so instantly obsessed with the sea that he had even gone as far as renting out his bungalow at the top of Westdene near the outskirts of the city and moving directly onto the seafront and into the top floor flat at number five, First Avenue, Hove – a building he had inherited from his deceased parents when he was barely a child and which until now had been mostly rented out.

Within the last few months, he had moved home, started a relationship and become an accepted member of the 7am sea swimming crowd. All because of a dream.

"Morning, Jesse," James said as he walked into the changing room.

Jesse dropped his bag on the bench in his usual corner and started to change into his trunks, without acknowledging James's welcome.

"You all right, mate?" James asked.

"He's not a morning person," Little Bob joined in.

"Ha ha," Jesse replied, a smile spreading on his face. "Sorry, I was miles away. Crap night's sleep, again."

"You say that every morning," Ben said.

"Yeah, well, it's because it always is."

When they were ready, the men waited in the hallway until the ladies joined them and then they all headed out as one pack down the pebbly beach to the sea's edge. At nearly ten degrees Celsius in the water and six degrees in the air, it was just about warm enough for Jesse, James and a couple of the others to swim all the way around the pier while everyone else stayed nearer to the edge, but on mornings like this, it was impossible not to stand and watch the sunrise before they set off.

At these temperatures, it was considered freezing cold for normal people, and even the daily sea swimmers could feel the temperature immediately seep into their skin. With the temperature of the sea still under ten degrees, some of the swimmers could only be in for a few minutes before the pain started to numb their bodies enough to make them head back to shore. Others, who carried more weight or a stronger mindset, were able to stay in a little longer.

Jesse stood ankle-deep in the water, his feet going numb, and decided that even the fish would wrap themselves up in scarves and hats in these temperatures if their brains were big enough to remember the cold. But despite the chilling air and the freezing water, he couldn't help but marvel at how beautiful the morning was – it was without a doubt becoming his favourite time of the day.

The swimming club's changing room, known as 'the arch', was situated in a perfect place to enjoy the best of the Brighton coastline. To the west of where they were standing was the Brighton Palace Pier, its stanchions providing a criss-cross view over to the ruins of the old burnt-out West Pier that was now no more than a monument of rust, and then onto the majesty of the gleaming British Airways i360, a 162-metre observation tower that provided visitors with breathtaking views along the south coast.

And to the east lay Brighton Marina, once simply a safe haven for sailors from the raging seas but now with all the restaurants, shops and fancy homes it was more like a small village in its own right than an extension of the seafront.

Brighton was truly a city of many faces.

At 7am it was still a little dark, and despite the light being thrown out by the sun rising up over the marina in the east, the moon was still visible over the i360 to the west, giving the seafront a feel as if it were in a science fiction movie with two moons sharing the same sky.

The coast also had a fine haze hanging over it, the air absolutely still and the sea completely flat, giving the illusion of an ice rink stretching as far as the eye could see. Standing to the left of the pier in around two feet of water, Jesse and his swimming friends made an odd picture to anyone happening to look down from the seafront above. There were ten of them that morning – Jesse, Ben, James, Geoff, Little Bob, David, Bryan, Jane, Midgie and Lindy – and they stood absolutely still looking towards the sunrise. Ten different shapes, ten different sizes, but each wearing the same orange club caps. Apart from new boy Jesse, the others were all long-standing members of the Brighton Sea Swimming Club who swam in the sea every day of the year; all of them crazy enough to stand there without a wetsuit, and all there for reasons that only a sea swimmer could understand.

"You fancy swimming around the pier, Jesse?" James asked him.

"Don't know. You?" Jesse generally liked to let James take the lead as he was far more experienced in the ways of the tides having been a member for over ten years.

"I don't think so, actually. It looks pretty flat but there's a huge undercurrent and I reckon it'll be a real battle at the head of the pier. And to be honest, I had a late night and am not sure if I can be bothered. What about just going out to the steps? What do you think?"

Jesse didn't hear James's reply. His attention had been drawn to a small rowing boat bobbing around just past the café halfway up the pier with a single female occupant leaning over the side staring into the water. It had seemed to come out of nowhere and was now drifting close to the pier and looked to be heading underneath the stanchions to the other side. Jesse fixed his eyes on the boat, wondering if the lady holding the two oars knew that while the gap was wide enough to take her through, it would only take a single rogue wave to smash the wooden boat against the pier and sink her in seconds.

"Let's just swim to that boat and see if she's OK. It's stupid being out there so early and so close to the pier."

"What boat?" James replied, seeing nothing. But Jesse had already dived into the sea and was heading out. James quickly went under and swam after him, trying to catch up but not quite managing it.

★★★

Walking up the beach after his swim, Jesse headed back to the arched doorway of the clubhouse, home to the Brighton Sea Swimming Club since the mid-1800s.

He swiped his waterproof fob against the reader and the door popped open, allowing him in. The entrance led to two separate changing areas, one on each side of the hallway; the right side for the men and the left for the women, each room complete with wooden benches, hot showers and hardworking radiators. It was all the swimmers needed after a cold morning swim.

"Shower's free, mate."

"Cheers, Bryan," Jesse called out.

He was generally the last one into the shower as he preferred warming up naturally, where others just dived in, desperate to get rid of the shakes.

When he had first joined the club, Jesse would be one of the first under the hot water to try to still the shivers, but he soon realised that the rush of blood back to his hands and feet could be agonising and more times than not he would find himself getting lightheaded from the blood rushing back to his brain too quickly. Cold-water swimming definitely took some time to get used to. Nowadays, he treated swimming just like he treated the rest of his life; he simply took his time and never thought much beyond the next few minutes. People were always in such a rush, but Jesse, with no one to get home to and a job that was simply to fill up part of his week rather than to keep him fed, had no reason to dash about; he was more than capable of getting everything done in the fullness of time.

"Did you see James when you came back?" Jesse asked Bryan. "I thought he was following me but when I got to the buoy and turned around, he wasn't with me."

"I think he headed off around the pier with Ben."

"I thought he said he couldn't be bothered?"

"You know what he's like, mate, always has to push himself

to the limits. It's still too cold for me to go around if I'm honest."

"Are they still out there, then?"

"No, they were crazy fast. The tide shot them around and they were back in under twenty minutes. I think you were out for about half an hour, mate, way too long for me in these temperatures."

"I wasn't out that long; I was only about ten minutes at most."

"No, you weren't, Jesse! You were bloody ages. Everyone was a bit worried about you, actually, James was waiting for a while, but then one of the girls said she saw you coming up the beach so he left."

Jesse didn't know what to say. He was sure he'd only been out for a few minutes.

"I only swam to where that boat was, but when I got there it seemed to have gone. I went under the pier a little way looking for it but didn't see anything so turned back. No way that could have taken me more than ten minutes."

"Honestly, mate, you were a good half an hour." Already dressed, Bryan headed for the door. "You coming for coffee?" he asked.

"I guess so," Jesse called back from under the shower, his mind still trying to work out what the hell had happened to the time.

"Cool. See you up there."

"OK, will do," he replied.

***

My Coffee Story was the newest independent coffee shop that had opened closest to the pier and was serving the best coffee in the area. It had quickly become somewhere that the morning swimmers would gather after their swim and before heading off to start their days. Having a coffee after the swim had become a ritual; in fact, they often joked that the swimming got in the way of the coffee some mornings.

Once he was dressed, Jesse headed down the hallway to the exit, stopping to look at the pictures lining the wall; he was always fascinated by the pictures of sea swimmers from the club's hundred-plus-year history. Swimmers old and new, different swimming costumes and different faces, but the sea was always there, unchanged, the one constant in them all. This morning it was the photograph of the five men standing in the sea during a low tide that caught his attention. With their stoic eyes, arms crossed and backs straight, they looked like they had just returned from a successful battle. Four of the men from the photo had been there at the arch this morning with him, perhaps that was why it had caught his attention, he wasn't sure, but something this morning struck him about the photo that he had not noticed before. He looked more closely at the five figures. Four he knew almost intimately having swum with them so often, but he had never met the fifth one, Adam Austin. He had drowned a few years before Jesse had joined the club. Adam was rarely spoken about at the club; he had drowned during an unexpected storm, some in the press even suggested it was possibly suicide that had made him go out that morning – the police and the swimming club had very different opinions on that.

Jesse had seen these pictures every morning since joining the club a few months back, but this morning his instincts had made him stop and take notice of it, especially of Adam Austin. There was something about the picture, almost a familiarity that he shouldn't have with this stranger, which made the hair on Jesse's neck stand to attention. He leaned in closer and for the first time looked beyond the men and noticed the background where the sun had risen in the east and the moon was still fixed to the west, and the mist was hovering over the sea like an old net curtain. He realised that the picture, while five years old, could easily have been taken just an hour ago. It was exactly like this morning, almost a carbon copy. In fact, it was so accurate that it could have been him rather than Adam standing next to James outside the arch.

As he continued to stare at the five men, he noticed in the background a small dot near to the pier. He leaned in closer to the frame and tried to make it out. It was so small he could hardly focus, but he was sure it was a little wooden fishing boat. He stepped back and looked again at the men. Each of them were looking straight ahead at the camera except Adam Austin. He was turning to look at the little boat.

Suddenly Jesse felt lightheaded and his vision started to blur. He shook his head to try to clear it, had to lean his hands against the picture to steady himself and close his eyes to stop feeling sick. When he opened them again, the face of the fifth man was no longer looking back to the sea, it was staring forward, straight at him. His eyes were like sparkling emeralds, piercing green even from such a small photograph and they seemed to be reaching right into Jesse's soul, desperately trying to tell him something. Jesse couldn't stop himself leaning in closer once again, until his nose was touching the frame and his own eyes started to blur at the closeness. The hairs on his arms stood erect and he felt as if someone had walked over his grave as an ominous feeling of déjà vu scuttled through him. He stepped back from the photo as a sense of deep sadness overwhelmed him and tears started to form. He squeezed his eyes shut as tight as he could before opening them again. The face was no longer staring forward, it was once again gazing out to the small wooden fishing boat by the pier.

No longer wanting to be in the arch, Jesse grabbed his bag off the floor and rushed outside onto the seafront into the fresh air. He breathed in deeply, trying to dispel the unease before striding purposefully up to the coffee shop, letting the cold air dry away the tears that had not quite escaped. He walked away from the beach with a purpose, not sure if what he had seen had been real or if it was just the cold water playing games with his head. What he needed right now was a strong coffee and some light banter with a friend; he really hoped James hadn't yet left for work.

"You took your time, Jesse," James remarked as Jesse slid onto the stool next to him.

"You know me," Jesse said. "Always the last to arrive."

"Did you put down the shutter when you left?"

Jesse thought for a second. "I can't remember actually."

"Someone left it open the other day as well. It's there for a reason, Jess!"

"I'm sure I shut it. Chill, Mr Club Secretary, all is well at the arch," Jesse said, hiding his unease and taking a sip of the small soya latte that had suddenly appeared in front of him.

"Good coffee today," Geoff commented, drawing 'Mmms' of agreement from the small group to his left.

"I've got to get going, actually, got a long day ahead of me," said Bryan as he picked up his bag. "See you, chaps, in the morning."

"I'll come as well," said Little Bob. "It's already half-eight and I've got to get a train to London today. See you tomorrow, chaps," he called to Geoff, James and Jesse as he followed Bryan out onto St James Street.

"So you swam around the pier after all?" Jesse asked, trying to find a way to gently broach a subject that he instinctively felt James would not want to discuss.

"Yes, Ben kind of challenged me. I tried to follow you, but you shot straight off so I caught up with Ben instead. Did you find that boat you thought you saw?"

"I did see a boat! It was gone, though, by the time I got there. She must have grabbed the tide and shot ahead."

"It was a strong tide out there for sure – massive pull to the west."

Jesse didn't want to talk about the boat, he wanted to get James on to the subject of Adam Austin.

"You've been a member of the club now for what, nearly ten years?"

"A little more than that, actually."

"So you knew Adam Austin quite well, then?"

"As well as anyone, I guess. A great guy. You would have liked him. He stood out – a bit like you do. Very popular with the ladies as well. If he hadn't been married with kids…" he trailed off.

Jesse realised that James had been disturbed by the memory of losing his friend and decided it was best to give it a few seconds before he carried on.

After a minute or so, he pressed on, hoping he wasn't going too far, but desperate to get the conversation back on track.

"I was looking at the picture of you all in the arch earlier. I'd never really looked closely at Adam before. What do you think made him do it? I mean going into such a crazy sea on his own?"

"I try not to think about it much these days if I can help it, you know, he was a good friend, and going back in the sea after he drowned…" James clearly found it hard finishing the sentence. "I think it made us all more respectful of the sea after that. Even Little Bob doesn't go into crazy seas these days, and apart from you, none of us would go in alone any more, not even in the weakest storm."

Jesse ignored the dig at him and pressed on. "Wasn't there talk of a suicide letter or something?"

"It wasn't suicide," James said with an edge to his voice. "The police didn't know him like we did, he was a really good guy; a family man, always happy, really good fun. It wasn't suicide, no way. They were wrong, simple as that."

"But there was a letter, wasn't there?"

James ignored the question and drank down the last of his coffee, putting the cup down on the table slightly harder than he usually would.

Jesse felt the change in James's demeanour.

"Sorry, I didn't mean anything by it. I was just saying, you know, it was just what the papers said."

"It's nearly quarter to and I've a patient in at nine-thirty. Best get going. See you in the morning, Jesse, and stay safe, mate."

"James, sorry, I didn't mean to stir anything up."

James didn't say anything else. He just picked up his bag and headed out into the busy street.

Jesse could always sense when something wasn't right; it was a gift he had, or a curse as he often called it.

He thought back to when he first woke up. It was the middle of the night and he had woken in a sweat, again, having dreamt about the girl covered in blood. Then there was the rowing boat he had swum to earlier that had seemingly vanished into thin air as soon as he had reached it, and then finally the photo in the arch. All random things, all unconnected, but something in the pit of Jesse's stomach told him otherwise.

He'd had lots of these moments throughout his childhood. Dreams that were so frighteningly real and feelings that came out of nowhere and rooted him to the spot. He suspected that even as a very young child he suffered from them, but it was only after his parents and twin sister had died that he could recall the pain of waking in the night completely petrified of something unknown, a feeling of dread that tore into him. Any real memories he had only started from after their deaths; there was nothing before that, just emptiness. It was as if his memories had only begun when his family had died.

He needed to talk to someone about the picture and there was only one person with whom he could talk honestly.

She lived too far away to walk there, so he headed back down St James Street just as the next bus pulled into the stop.

CHAPTER THREE

Jesse

"I can't explain the picture, Jesse, maybe you were tired from the swim or the light in the club was bad. I want to know more about the dreams, I think the key to all this is your dreaming."

"The light was bad; honestly, is that the best you can do?"

"I'm just saying that our eyes can play tricks on us."

"And my dreams are mind tricks as well, I assume. You're the one who keeps telling me there's more to this and now you're telling me it's all in my head."

"I never said that," Marlene replied, exasperated at Jesse's refusal to listen properly to her. "I am sure something happened in the club, but we've been working on your dreams for weeks now and I just don't want us to lose focus. Let's come back to the picture and the club later and for now just focus on the dreams."

"What do you want to know that I haven't already told you?"

"Well, you always tell me what you see but never what you feel. So tell me that; what did you feel in the dream?" Marlene asked him.

"It was the same dream as it always is, there's nothing more I can tell you. I want to talk about what happened at the beach today."

"We'll get there, Jess, I promise we will. Just trust me, OK. I need to know about the dream you had last night first; if it's still the same recurring dream then it might be someone trying to come through, a spirit, someone who needs your help."

"For Christ's sake, Marlene, you know I hate it when you talk like that, getting all theatre-like on me!"

"If you want my help then you have to take me as you find me. And I can't help you if you won't be specific when I ask you a question, Jesse. I've told you before, I need to know what you felt – I need to know how it felt physically, mentally and spiritually."

Ever since he'd met Marlene the previous year when he'd been dragged to one of her spiritual evenings by a girlfriend, she'd been pushing him to use his 'gift' as she called it. But to him it was a curse that had plagued him all his life. He would dream about people he didn't know in minute detail and would wake up with emotions he couldn't process. He'd have dreams from which he'd wake up screaming night after night, leaving him exhausted and troubled during the day. His foster family had put it down to the car crash that had killed his parents and twin sister when he was just a child and they assumed that his nightmares centred around them, but it was never them he dreamt about. He would have given anything to dream about his family, but he never did.

He could recall the night he met Marlene so clearly. He had walked alone into the Theatre Royal in Brighton, half an hour after the show had started, and it had been a walk that had changed his life forever.

Marlene Woolgar was a world-renowned spiritualist, one of only a handful in the world who managed to fill up theatres wherever she went. At sixty-two years of age, she still had the energy and charisma of a thirty-something. She held spiritual evenings in cities all around the world with her unique blend of mediumship and honesty, reaching out to an audience desperate for news of a loved one or an audience just wanting to believe. She would take them on a journey with stories that told of both her successes and her failures. Marlene's shows were as much about discovering the lies as they were about uncovering the truth. And it was because of this that every theatre she played in would be full and, in more cases than not, the reviews would be positive. This particular evening, she was returning to her home county of Sussex, and the Theatre Royal Brighton was alive with expectation.

Jesse was led into the auditorium by an usher and directed to the third row back in the stalls to the last empty seat in the building, next to his girlfriend. He stood for a second, wondering if he should scoot down the row making everyone stand up to let him in or if he should just turn back around and go out from where he had just come. Marlene's voice stopped him having to make the choice.

Unlike a usual theatre show, the lights were up full so Marlene could interact with her audience. Jesse stood briefly at the end of the row, embarrassed that every eye now seemed to be focused on him. His girlfriend, knowing how he hated being the centre of attention, couldn't help but catch his eye and throw him a shrug, blaming it on him for being late once again.

"Jesse?" Marlene asked, walking to the front left of the stage, turning her attention, and that of the audience, to him.

Her tone suggested that she knew him and hadn't seen him for so long that she wasn't sure it was really him. The audience took her tone as an assumption that they must surely be friends.

He nodded slightly, turning to face her, part of him wanting to believe that this was just a set-up, a part of her act, but at the same time he was unable to shake the feeling of déjà vu, his spider sense warning him that something important was about to happen. He stared at her for a few seconds, looking deep at her as if they shared each other's memories.

Jesse nodded again, this time with more certainty. He stood stock still, locking his eyes into hers while the eager eyes of the eight hundred other people in the auditorium were torn between the two of them.

"I've a message from your dad," she said matter-of-factly.

The moment she'd mentioned his dad, she'd broken the spell. All he could now see before him was just another cheap trick used to get vulnerable people sucked into the theatre of it all. He turned around, swept through the side curtain, pushed the handle down on the exit door and stormed out, letting the door slam behind him to the release of eight hundred held breaths.

He kept walking until he was out of the theatre and across the road, where he leaned against the railings to the Royal Pavilion Gardens and breathed in the salty evening air that rushed up from the beach just a few hundred metres down the road. It was already dark at seven-thirty and the city centre had the usual buzz of a Friday night, but he was oblivious to all the noise that surrounded him.

He had been standing there for over an hour before he felt a presence close behind him. He slowly turned around, instinctively knowing it would be her.

"Jesse, I knew you wouldn't run away. Your dad told me you'd wait for me."

Marlene stood behind him and placed her hands on his shoulders in comfort, understanding that just those words spoken out loud would cause him pain.

"Who the hell are you, and what was that stunt you pulled?" he said as he shrugged off her hands.

"It wasn't a stunt, Jesse. I don't do that sort of thing. As soon as you walked into the theatre, I knew your name, it was just in my head."

"What the hell does that even mean?" Jesse rounded on her, his anger getting the better of him.

"You know exactly what it means. You're like me, Jesse, I can feel it. You have the gift."

He turned to walk away but Marlene once again reached out her hand, this time with more force.

"I can help you."

"Help me! Who says I need help?"

"Your father does."

"My father's dead!"

"I know that. He told me you needed me. I want to help."

Jesse stood for a second, looking intently at Marlene and trying to work out if he should just turn and carry on walking or if he should scream at her to leave him alone.

He did neither.

"Let me help you, Jesse."

"Why, what do you want?" his anger settling at last.

"Nothing. I just want to help."

"Why, is it money? Do you think I'm an easy touch or something?"

The suspicion in his voice was clear for her to hear, it was something she had got used to over the years when she reached out to people in pain.

"Easy touch, after you stormed out of the theatre? Hardly."

"Then why?"

"I don't know. Maybe because I can sense you are different from other people. Maybe because I was like you once, someone with a gift and no idea how to use it. Or maybe because your father asked so nicely. I couldn't charge you, Jesse, your dad would be less than happy with me and he is rather persuading, isn't he?" she said with a wry smile on her face.

★★★

"Jesse, I need you to tell me what you felt before you woke up. Was your dream about the young girl again?"

"Yes, it was her – the same girl."

He closed his eyes and leaned back into the chair, trying to recall as much of the dream as he could. Usually, he could recall more about how he felt after the dream, feelings such as pain and anger, or happiness and laughter, rather than the physical details of what he saw, and it was always as the third person, never as a participant. But last night's dream had been different.

"I don't remember seeing much, I never do. I knew it was her straight away, though, I could feel her innocence, her childlike manner. When I first started dreaming about her a few months back it felt a bit false, almost like *someone* was trying to force me to watch her, and each time I pushed her away, I felt a resistance, as if someone was pushing back against me."

"So, what changed last night?"

"I did what you told me to do, I stopped resisting her. Although, I don't think it was the girl herself trying to contact me. Actually now that I think about it I'm not sure it was ever her – until last night. It's too hard to explain."

"Just use whatever words you can find, Jesse."

"OK, well, usually, it is like someone else is sending her message to me. I guess the best way I can describe it is like someone forwarding on an email to me from another person. The message is the girl's, but someone else was sharing it with me. And bit by bit, I started to feel more, like I was intruding on her feelings, but I didn't want to, it's like snooping on her, on her private thoughts, so I would always just push back, force them away. But last night it was different. It was like she was actually with me, the girl herself, physically with me, standing close to me, wanting me to come and save her, but at the same time she was scared of leaving someone else. Does any of that even make sense?"

"Describe what you were feeling to me. Everything you felt."

"I'm not sure I can. I think… I can't, it's just too hard to describe."

"Don't think, Jesse. I've told you so many times, you need to feel, not think. Close your eyes for me and draw back those feelings you had when you dreamt about her at the beginning. Give me single words that describe it; happiness, fear, that sort of thing."

24

Jesse did as Marlene told him and closed his eyes and tried to take himself back to the previous few months.

After a short while, he felt himself relax in the chair, his head laying back as he brought the dreams back into focus.

"I can feel happiness and love, definitely. But also a loss – she lost someone close, someone special. There's laughter as well. She laughs a lot. There's something else, someone... she has a bond, a closeness with someone else; they're sharing something, something deep; a brother or a sister maybe."

"That's good, Jesse, not untypical of a young child's emotions. But you said before that something changed last night, can you explain that?"

"Yes, someone else was there last night with her. Someone other than a brother or sister. I don't mean physically; it was more like she was two people in one body. The new person, or personality if I call it that, was really powerful, completely dominating her thoughts."

"And you said last night something else happened as well. What was it you said exactly?" Marlene looked down at the notes she had secretly made while Jesse had had his eyes closed. *"But last night it was like she was actually with me, wanting me to come and save her. What do you mean by that? Save her from what? Or from who?"*

Jesse opened his eyes and looked at Marlene. He had to think for a few seconds before he could answer her. She sat back and allowed him the time he needed to formulate his response.

"It happened suddenly, no warning. I was asleep, not dreaming at all, then suddenly I was with her. I think I actually saw her, the girl, only briefly. I saw green eyes staring into mine and I felt her clinging to me fiercely. She was holding me so tightly as someone – something – else was trying to pull her away from me. Someone was taking her into a nightmare and I couldn't stop it. We held on to each other, it felt like we were fighting for her life. She was shaking so much. She was watching something I couldn't see and whoever, whatever, it was, was too strong for us both. Also, and this was so strange, it felt like a part of her wanted me to let her go, to let them take her back; it's hard to explain. And then I woke up, shivering. I felt wet as well. Not sweating as such, it wasn't like that. It was like I had something on me, something sticky, and sweet. Then it was gone and it was just me again."

"That feeling, the sticky feeling, was it the blood you keep telling me you see in your dreams?"

Jesse closed his eyes again and tried to recall the dream, he tried to picture it in his mind. Marlene could feel the tension grip the room as he summoned the dream back into his mind.

"That's it, Jesse, bring it back. Tell me what you are feeling. Let the memory form in your mind."

"I can't do it."

"Relax, Jess. Breathe deeply. Stop thinking, stop trying. Just be. Just let it happen."

Marlene let the silence hang for over a minute as Jesse tried to calm his breathing once more. Then with the gentlest and slowest of voices she prompted him again.

"Do you see the girl, Jesse, is she with you now? Where are you?"

"I can't see her," he replied, his voice dreamy and confused. "But the blood, I can smell the blood everywhere."

"Open your eyes, Jesse. Just in your dream, open your eyes and tell me what you can see."

"It's dark. There are candles fixed to the walls letting off a white flame. I can see shadows everywhere. The furniture is old, really old, hundreds of years. And I can smell the blood. There's a bed, in the corner. And a girl, a scared girl crouched on the floor. She's not the one who I'm here to see, though."

Jesse's voice rose in panic as in the dream he spun around in the cold dark room.

"The door's open, it shouldn't be open, I can see footprints in blood leading out of the room, I'm scared, I don't want to follow."

Jesse's breathing sped up and Marlene could sense the scared child he was becoming.

"You can follow them, Jesse, it's safe for you to follow the footprints," Marlene whispered into his ear, forcing him onwards.

"The blood's everywhere, it's sticking to me, it's on my feet, on my hands. She's there, she needs me…"

Marlene could sense real fear in Jesse's voice.

"Come back to me, Jesse. Come back to me." She put her hands on his shoulders and gently rocked him back and forwards.

He awoke with a start. His skin had gone pale and his breathing was laboured.

"It's OK, Jesse, you're safe. You're with me now, it was just a dream, it's OK, it's all OK."

She let him catch his breath, and the colour return to his face before she continued the questioning.

"What happened, Jesse?"

"It was the dream, the one I keep having."

"But you said last night it was different; how so?"

"Last night the door actually opened. And then I was no longer in the seventeen or eighteen hundreds, I was now in my own time. And the girl was on the other side of the door looking at me. But there was someone else there as well, pulling her from outside. A lady, she was beautiful; pale skin that was almost translucent. She was pulling the girl towards her. But the girl took my hand and clung on to me as the lady pulled her. I tried to stop her from going, but suddenly she looked me in the eyes and then she smiled and let me go, sending herself into the lady's arms."

"And?"

"And I think I've seen her before, the lady." That stopped Marlene in her tracks.

"Can you describe them both to me, the girl at the door, and the lady you say you've met before?" she asked in a whisper.

"The girl was young, perhaps ten or eleven, and quite slight in build. She had light hair, almost blonde and a really pretty face. But she was so scared that it was hard to see beyond that."

Marlene looked down at her notes again.

"You said you saw her eyes. You said they were green?"

"Yes, I remember that, very briefly we locked eyes. A flash, that's all. And they seemed so familiar."

"In what way familiar?"

"I don't know," he said, exasperated.

"Have you seen her before, maybe in a book, or a picture?"

"Yes, a picture." Suddenly Jesse was upright and animated. "I've seen her eyes in a picture. But they were his eyes, not hers."

"His?"

Marlene could see an expression of doubt start to cross Jesse's face as the words slowly stopped.

"Who is he?" Marlene's words were delivered slowly in a monotone, trying to encourage him to go deeper into his mind again.

"They're having an affair," he said as soon as he opened his eyes. "Who are?" asked Marlene, now utterly confused.

"The lady, the one who took the girl in my dream. I've seen her before as well, at the beach this morning. She's having an affair. He's a married man and she works for his wife and him. They own a hotel on the seafront. The wife took her in, treats her like family, but she's having an affair with her husband…"

"This is this the girl from your dream? I'm confused now."

"What, no, God, no. The girl in my dream is just a child."

"I don't understand. Who are you talking about then?"

"The lady who took the girl away from me, she's the same lady from the boat this morning. I swam to her near the pier; she was all alone. Then she was gone, or at least I thought she was gone. But I just saw her again, just now in my dream. As I came to my senses, I had a flash of what happened this morning. I was at the beach with the guys. I swam over to her, and I thought she had gone. But she hadn't gone, she was there, but until now I didn't remember what I'd seen. Bryan said I'd been gone longer than I thought I had; he was right. I somehow must have fallen into a dream when I was swimming, if that's even possible. But I've seen her again, just now, and I think I know her name."

"Seen who, Jesse, who is she?"

"The lady in the boat. She's the same lady in my dream, the one who's pulling the young girl away from me. And she is the one having the affair. Her name is Lilly. And there was someone else in the sea with her; a man?"

Jesse closed his eyes for a second to recall the memory.

He continued, "There was a man in the sea and she was rowing the small boat next to him, following him as he swam. His name's John. And they were having an affair."

"Who are they, Jesse? And what's their connection to the young girl in your dreams?"

Jesse suddenly sat up, no longer narrating someone else's story from his mind, but firmly back in the room. Marlene saw the distress in his eyes as he returned to her.

"You say you saw all that this morning?" she asked him incredulously.

"No. Well, I mean, I must have done, I'm not sure."

"What exactly happened, Jesse? Tell me what happened." Marlene had to push now as she was losing his attention. "Is the young girl in your dreams and this lady the same person? Is that what you felt?" Marlene was grasping at straws trying to keep Jesse talking.

His face suddenly turned pale as it dawned on him.

"No. The lady in the boat and the girl, they are different, but… but I felt something… something else. It was the same energy pushing me away in the dream just now that was last night pulling the young girl into the nightmare. The lady in the boat is connected to the child I keep dreaming about and she was there last night in my head, dragging the child into her nightmare."

"And the man? You called him John. You said they were having an affair. Who is he?"

Jesse stood up, grabbed his coat and phone from the chair next to him and headed for the door.

"Jesse!" Marlene called out after him.

"I need time. I'll come back tomorrow, I promise,' he called back as he pulled the door open.

"Jesse, who are they, you called her Lilly? Lilly who? Jesse, I can't help you if I don't understand!"

"I don't know who she is," he called back. "But it's connected, it's all connected."

He slammed the door shut behind him and ran as fast as he could to the bus stop, leaving Marlene with snippets of stories that made no sense at all, but which left her feeling sick to her stomach.

CHAPTER FOUR

Natalie

Breakfast was just a series of smiles, grunts and affirmations. "Alfie, I'm talking to you. Daisy. Hello, Mum calling Daisy. Either of you!"

It exasperated Natalie that she had to fight so hard to get the twins to say anything with her.

Before she lost Adam, the Austin family would talk about and share everything. No stone was ever left unturned and no sentence was ever finished by the person who had started it. Natalie had loved that about her family. As babies, the twins were happy to go to either her or Adam – there was no daddy's girl or mummy's boy in their household. When they started school, Natalie had insisted that the twins were in separate classes as she wanted to make sure that they formed their relationships and didn't just rely on each other, which the school were happy to support. It meant that they built their own group of friends so that when they got home each night the family could sit around the table over dinner and each share exactly what they had done that day; often starting with *what I had for breakfast* and ending with *and you know the rest*. It had become an Austin family tradition that every meal was eaten together and every meal included the *what I did* course.

It had all stopped the day Adam didn't come home from his swim.

Natalie had tried her best to keep everything together, but to begin with the emotion of losing her soulmate, her best friend, was simply too much to take. If not for the kids, she doubted she would have had the strength or the desire to carry on living. Having children meant there was no choice. But it had been a battle and the twins had to find their own way of dealing with their loss. So, they inevitably found each other again. It had started off as a simple need to be near each other, just to be close was enough to comfort them. The school had dealt with the fallout as best they could and, after a few blowouts, they had spoken to Natalie and all agreed that at least for the time being it would perhaps be best if Daisy was moved to Alfie's class. This one move had helped them both so much that it had never felt right to then try to separate them again.

At home, it was much the same. The day after Adam's body had been found, the three of them had fallen asleep on the one bed, all comforting each other. But after a few nights, Natalie had decided that it wasn't healthy to all be sleeping in one bed and she encouraged them back into their own rooms. But it had been too much for them; there was no way they could sleep apart. Natalie, desperate for sleep and craving quiet, agreed quickly that Daisy could move into Alfie's room and they could get bunk beds. That was five years ago and Daisy's room had not been slept in since. Natalie doubted it would change until the teenage years set in and privacy became an essential rather than an inconvenience.

It wasn't only the sleeping arrangements that had changed. The twins had formed such a strong bond that Natalie found herself very much on the outside. No longer did the Austin family share their day over dinner and it was perhaps no more than once a week that Natalie could find the energy to force them all to eat together. The times they did sit at the table as a family, like breakfast this morning, the twins would talk amongst themselves and offer Natalie only the crumb of a grunt or a nod. Natalie knew that it wasn't that they didn't love her, or that they had in some way blamed her for their dad's death; it was simply that they didn't need her. What they needed was a nanny or a maid and Natalie had slotted into that role so quickly and efficiently that it had all happened without her even realising.

"Guys, please, just for once can you give me an answer that is more than just a shrug. For Christ's sake you're nearly ten years old, surely you can hold down a conversation with me now."

"Sorry, Mum," they said in unison without looking up from their iPads. "And put the bloody iPads away, how many times have I told you I don't like them at the table when we eat."

Alfie and Daisy looked at each other and shrugged before turning them off and pushing them into the middle of the table.

"Thank you," Natalie said, pleased that at least that battle was quickly over. "So, what was the bad dream about, Daisy?" she asked.

"I didn't have a bad dream," Daisy replied innocently.

"I heard you scream out."

"No, I didn't."

"She didn't, Mum," Alfie chipped in.

"I heard what I heard. You screamed something. It was about three in the morning. I came in as quickly as I could, I couldn't find my glasses. When I got there you and Alfie were both fast asleep, together."

"Ah, OK, you must have heard me climbing down the ladder, that was all."

"That's right, Alfie woke up and was talking to me so I told him to come down so we didn't wake you up."

"You screamed out, Daisy, I heard you."

"I never did," Daisy said, grabbing Alfie by the sleeve. "Come on, Alf."

They were gone before Natalie could stop them, their breakfast half eaten and the conversation unfinished.

"I know what I heard!" Natalie called out to them.

She knew she shouldn't blame herself for the fact that she'd let it get like this, but when Adam had died, part of their family unit had died with him.

Over the last couple of years, her friends, who had been *their* friends, had tried to introduce her to 'eligible' partners, but for Natalie, five years was not long enough to start again. For her it felt like a lifetime would have to pass before she could even think about anyone else in a romantic way. The fact that she still had Adam's business bringing her in a decent income also meant she didn't need anyone else in that sense either. Her priority was the twins and her own needs would always come way down the list as far as she was concerned.

★★★

Out in their own back garden, Daisy and Alfie climbed to the treehouse and sat on the platform that hung over the trampoline, their legs dangling.

"Tell me what Lilly showed you last night," Alfie asked his sister.

"I don't want to talk about her, Alf, it wasn't nice."

"Who else was in there?" he asked.

"What do you mean?"

"When you screamed it was like you were calling to someone to help you."

"Oh yes," she said, thinking back. "I'd forgotten he was there. He was trying to help me, he was holding me really tightly, but Lilly was too strong for him. She can be really strong. Shall we play with the frisbee?"

"Sure," Alfie said, letting Daisy end the conversation first as she always did.

CHAPTER FIVE

Jesse

In his dream, Jesse was a child again. He was in the family car, driving through France with his sister and his mum and dad all squeezed on to the back seat while he sat in the front next to the driver. At first, he couldn't make out who the driver was, but as his eyes focused, he could see it was a young lady with very pale skin and shoulder-length hair. Without even seeing her face, he knew it was the lady he had swum to in the boat, the same lady who had been haunting the young girl in his dreams. It was Lilly. She drove furiously, looking away from him the whole time, her blue eyes focused only on the road, not once looking to her side. His parents and sister sat in the back quietly smiling and saying nothing. He screamed at Lilly to stop and begged her to slow down. But she just looked straight ahead, her eyes locked on the road, as she drove at extreme speed towards the edge of the mountain. He woke up in a sweat, his heart beating at a hundred miles an hour as his phone rang harshly into the room, breaking him from the dream before the car left the road, killing them all.

He grabbed his watch from the side, his eyes trying to adjust. Nine o'clock. He had missed his seven o'clock swim. He had broken his routine. Instantly, the guilt of not swimming hit him like a sledgehammer. He grabbed the phone in frustration at its insistent ringing; his throat was parched and he found he was unable to speak clearly.

"Jesse, are you there? Jesse?" the voice shouted at him.

"Pete?" Jesse croaked.

"Where the hell are you, man? You bloody promised you would open the shop today. You know I needed to take the kids to school. Claire told me you wouldn't turn up, but as usual I defended you and once again my wife was right. Just one bloody morning, Jesse, I promised her I'd take the kids just this one morning so she could go and help her mum. You know her dad's on his last legs."

"Oh shit, sorry, Pete. I had a really bad night; I didn't sleep a wink."

"Who gives a shit, man. I don't know why I bloody bother with you."

"I'm on my way." Jesse spoke into a dead line, leaving his guilt to quadruple. "Shit."

"Who was it?" Susie asked, waking up to the noise.

Jesse had forgotten he was in Susie's flat again. In truth, he couldn't even have explained how he had ended up there if someone had asked him.

"My brother. I promised to be at the shop to help out but look at the time."

"Well, there's nothing you can do about it now, is there? My restaurant doesn't open until lunchtime, so stay a bit longer? Maybe, you know, we can carry on from where you fell asleep," she added suggestively.

"I really can't, I promised Pete I would open up the shop for him. And I told James I would swim around the pier this morning with him. And I've missed both." He rolled out of bed and started to pull on his jeans. "I really need to get to the shop and put it right with him."

"It's a fucking bike shop, Jesse. So, it opened an hour late today, who really cares? And so James swam on his own for once. I'm really getting fed up with you just turning up when you want and then running off first thing."

"Yes, I get it, Susie, I'm sorry, OK. Look, I've let Pete down again and I really feel like shit about it. He's always been there for me, and I always seem to let him down. I've got to go over and put it right."

"And what about letting me down!" she screamed as he left the bedroom.

He was almost out the door and cycling along the seafront before her words had left her mouth.

★★★

Jesse hated missing his morning swim, but he hated letting his foster brother down even more.

As a child of just eight, Jesse had nearly lost his life along with his entire family. Somehow, by some miracle, as the car careened off the mountain in Provence, France, he had been thrown clear and was found barely conscious by a group of cyclists who were slowly making their way to the peak. They managed to get him, and themselves, clear of the wreck before it burst into flames, killing his parents and his sister instantly.

After establishing his identity, the local gendarmes managed to contact his father's business partner in London who had immediately flown over and gone straight to the hospital. What followed was a quick process; the car crash was classed as a tragic accident on a dangerous mountain and Jesse was taken back to London by his new foster family – a family Jesse had known through his dad's work, but not people he knew intimately enough to simply move in with. The following months had proved difficult for Jesse and his new family. They had done everything they could for him, but his erratic behaviour, his anger issues and his constant nightmares simply overwhelmed them all. They managed to keep him with them until he was sixteen, a period of their own lives that they would never wish on anyone else, and then on the day of his sixteenth birthday, without so much as a thank you, he packed a few clothes, grabbed as much cash as he could from the house and headed away from London, and back to his former home city of Brighton.

For many years, Jesse had not appreciated how well his foster family had looked after him, especially Pete's father who, out of loyalty to his business partner, had converted, at his own expense, Jesse's family home into six large flats and let them all out, creating a huge income for the young Jesse, as well as protecting Jesse's shares in the business so that he was now a fifty-fifty partner with Pete and Pete's sister Rosie in the London theatre that their fathers had jointly and successfully run for many years. It wasn't until Jesse had reached his thirties that he realised just how much he had owed to his foster parents, something he knew he should have told them at every given chance, but so many years had passed so quickly that he had never quite found the right words; it was a regret he would always harbour. Throughout all this, his foster brother Pete had never lost touch with him; he was the one person in Jesse's life who had never questioned or judged him. The same could not be said for his foster sister Rosie who had been glad to see the back of him all those years ago and still resented having to share the family business with him.

Pete was the only person he could rely on. And once again he had let him down.

Jesse cycled along the seafront heading straight from Susie's flat to Pete's shop in Rottingdean, a small town on the outskirts of Brighton, to try to smooth things over. As he rode past the pier, he couldn't help stopping on the pavement and going right up to the balustrade that sat directly above the swimming club arch. Despite being in a rush to get to Pete's shop, he still found himself so drawn to the sea that he was unable to stop himself getting off the bike and gazing out to the spot where he had seen Lilly's boat. He had hoped deep down that perhaps if he stood there long enough and concentrated really hard he could somehow magically bring her back right then, but he knew it was not how his gifts worked. He could see and feel things that others couldn't, he could even be taken by Marlene to places deep in his past, but he couldn't conjure things up at will.

And much as it pained him beyond words, he still hadn't found a way to reach out to the spirits of his own family to find out why they had died that night and left him alone on that dark, windy mountain. He shook the thought from his head and turned back to his bike when he spotted out of the corner of his eye someone walking out of the sea. He knew it had to be a swimming club member as only they would get into the sea at this time of day without a wetsuit on. Knowing he was already in Pete's bad books and that another half an hour would now make no difference at all to the trouble he was in, he let the curiosity as to who was swimming on their own at half past nine take preference. He chained his bike to the railing and quickly headed down the slope to the arch just as the swimmer appeared, their fob in hand ready to open the door.

"Hey, Jesse, what you doing down here at this time?" Geoff asked.

Geoff was a long-standing member of the Brighton Swimming Club and co-secretary with James. He was also a policeman with the local force and someone Jesse had a lot of respect for.

"I could ask you the same thing," Jesse replied, following Geoff into the arch.

"I've been on nights and was just heading home and couldn't resist a quick dip."

"I don't blame you; it looks beautiful."

"Didn't you swim this morning?"

"No, I overslept."

"Not like you, Jess."

"I know. I haven't been sleeping well recently and it's been hard to get up."

"Too much time on your hands, mate. You need to get a proper job, something that challenges you a bit more."

"I know, I know. Don't suppose there're any jobs in the police force, are there?" Jesse joked.

"I wouldn't do it to you, mate."

"Geoff, you were here when Adam Austin drowned, weren't you?"

"I wasn't actually here. But I was a club member, yes. Why?"

"Was it suicide? He left a letter, didn't he?"

"You OK, Jesse? You're not down or anything, are you?"

Jesse realised where Geoff was going with this and laughed. "God no! I'm way too conceited to commit suicide. No one really talks about him and, well, you know, it's interesting as a new member to try to understand what happened."

"Fair enough, mate. Actually, you know, we should talk about it more. Whether it was suicide or a tragic accident, we shouldn't ignore the dangers of the sea. And we shouldn't swim on our own – anything can happen."

"That's a bit like calling the kettle black, isn't it?"

"I guess so. But I don't usually swim on my own, this was a one-off for me."

"So was it like that with Adam? Maybe he went in on his own as a one-off and never expected to get caught in a storm?"

"Maybe. It's hard to say. It was stormy that day, though, and it was unexpected. And he did leave a note, although it was more of a letter to James than a suicide note."

"What did it say?"

"I can't remember it all. There's a copy somewhere. I'm sure it's available in the public domain. It was a bit rambling actually. He said he had to *go and stop her*, something about *going back*. We didn't really understand it as there was no one else missing. Anyway, the force classed it as suicide. It was odd, though, Adam always came across so carefree. But you never know people, do you."

"Interesting; maybe I'll look it up."

"Don't dig too deep, Jesse," Geoff warned him. "It's still a tough one for all of us down here and there are some – James especially, I think – who would like to let it lie."

"Understood," Jesse said.

Jesse got to the bike shop to find Pete looking less than pleased.

"I'm so sorry, Pete, really mate, I got waylaid and…"

"No, you're not sorry, Jesse, you never are," his foster brother replied as he put down the phone to a customer, just as another walked through the door.

"You're probably right," Jesse threw back as he walked past Pete, giving him a wink. "I'll start on fixing the old red Raleigh, shall I?"

"It needs new brakes and gears and the chain needs a good clean."

"Got it," Jesse called back.

"Arsehole!" Jesse heard Pete shout back at him, before hearing him apologise to the customer for his language.

Apart from being in the sea, fixing up bikes was the only other time that Jesse felt at peace; never more so than doing it in his brother's shop. But this morning, the conversation with Geoff about Adam's letter wouldn't leave his mind.

Had to go back. Had to stop her.

The words played around and around in Jesse's head as he started to pull the old chain on the Raleigh apart link by link.

CHAPTER SIX

Marlene

After her first meeting with Jesse, Marlene realised that her gifts as a spiritualist may be well developed compared to most but compared to him they were just scratching the surface. When she had first studied mediumship in her early twenties and developed her skills as a spiritualist, she had come across some teachers who believed that there were others out there who could do so much more than them; individuals who could manipulate time to the extent that they could literally time travel in their minds and witness events both past and future. Mostly the teachers retold old fairy tales and folk stories, but there had been one teacher in her earliest days who had told of, and fervently believed, in the legend of the ghost hunters. He would describe a group of people who had unlocked the mysteries of life after death, people he said held incredible power without having the wisdom to use it for the betterment of man. He believed it so much that he had wasted his entire career searching for, but never actually proving them. At the time she had dismissed him, as so many others did, as a crazy old fool. But something inside her now told her that Jesse was special, that maybe, just maybe he was the one her old teacher had spent his life searching for; the ghost hunter.

Soon after their first meeting, and with the stories of her old teacher rolling around her head, she had taken a fast train from

Brighton to London and then a taxi straight to the British Library. Once there, she had headed to the religious historical section and pulled out book after book on mediums and psychics and ancient religious cultures through the history of time. She was certain that somewhere in there would be a text or a book that could explain how she had felt when Jesse first walked into her show, maybe a picture even, that could explain why she felt what she felt.

During the first day, she spent over ten hours in the library and had learned nothing at all, just the same old lessons she had been taught decades ago. She had got the last train home and spent the whole journey trying to convince herself that going back would be pointless, that the feelings she had about Jesse were nothing more than a tired lady's fantasies that the old stories could be true. But when she awoke the next day, she knew she had to go back and try again; it was almost like she was being forced to do it by some invisible force. It was on this second day there that she found herself drawn not to the religious books but to the language section. She had no reason to be there other than a feeling in her gut guiding her room by room; *You're getting hotter*, it would say. *Hotter still, even hotter, whoa, you're on fire.* She instinctively bent down and thrust her hand forward, grabbing a book in front of her and gently easing it out. It looked like all the other books around it, solid and glossy, and displaying ancient languages on its jacket. But it was far too light to be a book of that size, it was almost paper thin, and weightless. Taking the book over to the table, she slowly opened it up, scared of what her instincts had led her to. Inside the cover there was a stack of papers instead of a bound book. There were only thirty pages in total and they were handwritten in an ink that had faded over the centuries, barely legible. The writing took some getting used to as the words were written in old Hebrew. After leaving school with very little in the way of exams and now heading close to retirement age, Marlene had in recent years decided to spend much of her time on a subject that always fascinated her and enrolled on numerous online courses studying ancient languages. Hebrew was one of the more complex languages she'd had to master, and although she could now read it fairly confidently, when it was written without the vowels under each letter it took her some time to decipher the words correctly. She knew it was not possible for her to break this book down in just one sitting.

The book had to have some great significance, otherwise why had she been drawn to it? She needed time to study it, but the library was about to close for the weekend and she was worried she'd never find it again.

As she walked down the stairs to the main exit gate, she could hardly believe that she had put the sleeve back on the spine, then the book back on the shelf, and quickly folded the loose papers into her boots for fear that the guard might check her bag and see them hidden there. Literally every step she was taking she was doing so along with papers that had been written thousands of years before; she almost smiled at the thought that she was literally walking in history.

A knock on the door brought her out of the memory. She let Jesse in and led him into the lounge, allowing him to naturally sit on the same chair he always chose, the one closest to the door. She found herself smiling at the fact that he always needed to be close to the exit.

It was already getting dark by the time Jesse had left the bike shop and the cycle from there to Marlene's house was mostly uphill, leaving him slightly out of breath.

"You OK, Jesse?" she asked as he took his seat.

"I'm fine, just need to catch my breath."

"So you came back."

"Of course."

"Yesterday, before you stormed out of here, you referred to the lady as Lilly. How did you know her name exactly?"

"That's exactly what I've come to ask you," Jesse replied.

"How could I know that?" she said. "Did you hear the name being spoken to you? Was it a voice speaking to you in a dream? Or did you just suddenly know?" Marlene tried to guide him to work it out himself.

"I just knew it, it just popped into my head like I've always known it."

Marlene could see his frustration as he sat back in the chair and let out a huge sigh. Her *training* sessions, as she called them, always frustrated him. She knew he so desperately wanted to believe her when she told him that this was a positive gift he had, but he was torn between not believing in it at all, despite having witnessed and felt spirits all his life, and being frustrated by never being able to be in contact with his dad, when Marlene herself seemed to be on first name terms with him. The grief of losing his family consumed every part of him and she desperately wanted to talk to him about it. But he would never share his tears with anyone, not even her.

She let him sit there for the next ten minutes in silence, before prompting him again.

"Jesse," she said in her quiet, encouraging voice.

"I can't find the words to explain it," he said, the frustration and emotion telling in his voice.

Marlene saw the battle raging in him as she always did.

"Jesse, we're similar, you and me. We can do things other people can't. If only you could separate your gift from your anger, embrace it like I do. If you let it, it can bring you more comfort than you could possibly imagine."

She could always see how he dealt with his pain, hiding it rather than facing it, but she needed to keep him focused now. She would deal with his anger later, but for now she needed to help him use his gift to share this story with her.

"You can't always explain it; sometimes it's just a feeling, I understand that. I've never had the visions you have, Jesse, I've never been in that cinema state you find yourself in. Mine is so much more basic than that. It's the same for all of us, except you."

"If I'm so bloody gifted then why can't I see my dad like you can?" It was a question he had asked her a hundred times.

"I can't see him either, Jesse. I can hear him, though, I've explained that to you. We don't get to choose. None of us do. They choose us. You're too close to your family, Jesse. It would be too much for you to handle, even for someone as gifted and strong as you. Your dad found me for a reason; you need to accept that's how it has to be."

"But what if I can't accept it? If I could hear him, or even sense him there... that's all I need. Just the once."

"I can't help you on that, Jesse. It's not how it works."

The anger resurfaced in a millisecond and Jesse sprang up from the chair like a fire was under him and headed for the door without looking back.

"You called her Lilly," Marlene called out to him. "Let me help you find out who Lilly is."

Jesse held the door open, undecided whether he should leave or stay.

"If you want to know about Lilly, who she was and why she's found her way into your life, then you had better get over this childish rant and sit down. Let's work this out together," she said as she took his hand and tried unsuccessfully to lead him back into the room.

She produced the old papers she'd stolen from the library and held them up to him as a way of tempting him back to his chair. "If you're right and this Lilly is somehow connected to the girl in your dreams, then we need to know who they both are and exactly what links them. Only you can do this, Jesse, and how you do it is in here," she said, holding the papers up higher for him to see.

Marlene quoted from the book without having to reread it – '*A vengeful ghost has powers in our dimension that we can't fully comprehend yet.*'

"Jesse, if you've been given her name, then it's because someone who has passed over *wants* you to stop her. Whoever it is speaking to you needs your help."

Marlene had stopped him in his tracks by showing him the old papers again. It was only the second time she had shown them to him. The first time she had sat him down and translated the words and they had taken his breath away. The author, whoever they were and whenever they had existed, seemed to have been able to describe feelings and understandings that he had, but had never been able to put into words. Even Marlene couldn't understand everything she'd read out to him, but somewhere, deep in his soul, he understood it all.

He came back into the room and she passed the papers to him. He had never been able to speak any language apart from English, even basic French and Spanish at school had been too much of a challenge. His brain simply had not been wired for languages. But the book had been different. The sweeping of the pen, the pictures making up shapes of dots and lines, the drawings and scribbles that for the most part looked like a baby's scrawl; somehow, they could reach down into him and bring up feelings and fears that he had never known existed. The first time she had shown it to him he had even corrected her on her translation.

"What is it?" she asked now as he read the first page. "It's different."

"Different? What do you mean different?" she asked as he took a seat next to her on the sofa.

"Last time, the first page was a story, wasn't it? The ghost hunter story. Look for yourself."

He passed her the text.

Marlene looked at the first page and read out what she saw. Jesse snatched the book back from her.

"Jesse!" she exclaimed.

"It doesn't say that! Look, it's changed." Marlene leant over him.

"It's exactly as it's always been," she said, bemused. She turned to him. "What are you seeing that I can't?"

"It's changed. When I look at the words it's as if they speak to me. I hear them, in my head."

"I don't expect to understand how you can read it, Jesse, I never will. To me, and I'd expect to anyone else who understands language, it's written in an ancient script, resembling Hebrew. Maybe it hides an ancient text in there that only your kind can understand," Marlene said as Jesse tried to put into words what he felt.

"My kind! You and I are the same *kind*, whatever that is," Jesse shot back at her.

"I don't think we are," she said. "Perhaps, I thought we were, right at the beginning, but the more time we spend together, the more I come to realise that we are separate ends of the same graph."

"And what's that supposed to mean?"

"I don't know, Jesse."

She sounded exhausted.

"Well, if we're so different, how the hell are you going to help me, then?"

"What is the book telling you?" she asked again.

"It's a story, similar to the one you first told me. It's still about a ghost hunter. But this time she's young. Inexperienced. She's not yet ready to face the demon."

Marlene smiled.

"It's you, Jesse. The book is telling you your own story."

Jesse thought for a moment. He looked back down at the pages. "There's more," he said. "She wants to fight. The demon is coming for her in her dreams and she wants to fight it. But there's something else, a teacher of sorts, next to her ear, screaming into her head."

"What's it screaming to her, Jesse?"

Jesse put the book down on his lap and leaned back into the sofa. "It's telling her to run."

"And did she?"

"Yes."

"And are you going to?" she asked. Again, Jesse sat in silence for a moment. "No," he said at last.

"OK, then, let's get to work," she replied as worry was etched on her face.

CHAPTER SEVEN

Jesse

The next morning, exhausted from a late night at Marlene's house and then a long cycle home in the dark, Jesse once again woke much later than usual. The digital clock by his bed beamed ten o'clock instead of its usual six o'clock. He rarely bothered to set his alarm as his body clock never let him down; this morning, though, he wished he had as he hated not getting to the beach before the tourists arrived. Having missed his early morning swim for the second time this week he decided there was no reason to rush now, so he stopped to grab a coffee from the Small Batch coffee shop around the corner. The session last night with Marlene had been mentally hard on him. He had been ready to walk away, but as usual, her tough talk had brought him back. He'd walked away from any number of friends and girlfriends in his life but walking away from Marlene was something he didn't have the strength to do. She was the only one who could help him make sense of anything, and she was the closest way he had of one day being able to reach his dad.

Having collected his latte from the counter, he slung his swim bag onto his back and started the short walk down the road and over to the pier. The morning was beautifully calm, the sky was a brilliant blue and there wasn't so much as a breeze disturbing the flags that lined the fronts of the hotels along the seafront. At almost half past ten, the seafront was already getting busy. The early morning runners had been replaced with strolling groups of students, and the 7am fitness freaks and their personal trainers who littered the lawns along the seafront every morning had been replaced by the more sedate dog walkers.

It took Jesse just twenty minutes to get to the arch. The front shutter was up, which meant that the later morning swimmers were still there. He knew a few of them by face and a couple by name, but mostly they were strangers to him; a nod and a smile was generally all that was exchanged between him and them. Swiping his fob against the door, it swung inward, inviting him in. The arch was deathly quiet, even the dripping tap seemed to be silent this morning. He picked up the diary by the sink and saw the dozen or so names from the early crowd; all his usual lot had been there, perhaps wondering why Jesse was missing once again. Then, further down, leaving a small gap between them, another name was scrawled; the letters were smudged, but the initials seemed to be AA. They hadn't yet signed out so no doubt whoever it was had raised the shutter and was either already in the sea or was walking down the beach right now.

Without warning, the temperature dropped and a menacing feeling of déjà vu crept over him. Wrapping his arms around himself, he breathed out, leaving cold vapour in the air. Now, he thought about it; he didn't know anyone at the club with the initials AA; maybe it was a new member. He looked around expecting to see a bag, because whoever it was, surely they'd have left a bag behind when they went for a swim. But there was nothing, not even dropped under the benches.

He walked back out of the men's and into the ladies' area, but it too was empty. The temperature was becoming unbearable, and he could feel his heart starting to thump hard against his chest. He had to get out of the arch before the panic overwhelmed him.

Fumbling in his haste, he changed quickly and tied his fob around the drawstring of his swimming trunks, pulled on his hat and headed to the door, goggles in hand. He stopped abruptly in the narrow hallway. Out of the corner of his eye, he had noticed something that seemed different. The framed sketch of Captain Webb, the first man to have swum the channel back in eighteen seventy-five, was hanging on the wall by the door. His brain told his eyes that something was wrong with this. There was something else usually in that spot, Captain Webb had never been hung here. Then it struck him. This had been where the last picture taken of Adam Austin had been hung. Jesse spun around trying to see where it had been moved to. But it wasn't anywhere. It had been taken down.

He couldn't deal with this right now; his head was starting to feel fuzzy from the cold and he needed some air and warmth on his face.

He swiftly left the arch, pulling the door closed behind him, and headed down the beach, letting the sun brush away the cold air that had been surrounding him. He threaded his way through the students and day trippers setting up for a morning on Brighton's most famous stony beach, keeping the calm of the sea firmly in his sights. He stepped out of his old grey crocs near the edge of the water and pulled his goggles down over his eyes.

With a deep sigh, he looked out to sea, trying to decide whether it was warm and calm enough to swim around the pier. He decided it was. With his destination set, he put his first foot into the water; something in the distance then caught his eye. By the first yellow buoy just 150 metres to the east of the pier, almost in line with the silver ball that jutted up into the sky, someone was swimming. He'd not expected to see anyone at this time. Whoever it could be was heading just around the buoy and turning west to swim along and under the pier. Jesse concentrated on the figure. While it was a distance out, he figured it was a man due to the long arm stretch on the front crawl. Also, he noticed that he was wearing a bright orange swimming club cap. It was essential for arch swimmers to wear a club hat so that they could be spotted in the water if a lunatic came roaring past kite surfing or on a jet ski and didn't see them bobbing about in the water.

Jesse strained his eyes in case he was mistaken, but it was definitely a club hat, he was sure of that. But who was it? He thought maybe it was the person in the diary, with the initials AA, but the arch had been empty, not even a bag on the bench or any clothes hanging off the hooks, and there wouldn't have been anyone out in the sea on their own unless they were a club member, not at this time of year with the temperatures still too low for the average person to be so far out in the sea.

He wanted to know who it was. He dived in and swam as quickly as he could towards the buoy. Most sea swimmers, especially the experienced ones in the arch, could reach two miles an hour in a flat sea like this, but Jesse, with his athletic frame and strong chest, could hit three miles an hour in most conditions. He reached the buoy quickly and turned himself west towards the pier.

But the swimmer had disappeared.

He twisted around in a circle in case the man had swum back and under the pier further down without him seeing, but there were no other orange hats bobbing about or heading away from the buoy. He twisted again and concentrated his vision towards the buoy on the other side of the pier to the west, expecting to see the swimmer there. But the sea was empty. All he could see through the stanchions was the burnt-out skeleton of the West Pier a mile away and the tall thin stick of the British Airways i360 rising up from the seafront.

Anxiety gnawed at his stomach. Without taking a single breath, he put his head down low into the water and completed twenty-one perfect strokes, taking a quick breath after each set of three, his head staying low, his legs high up and his shoulders turning with each thrust of his arm. He swam under the pier towards the other beach in the hope of spotting the swimmer on the other side. He broke through under the pier and looked around for the next yellow buoy; it wasn't there. It had been there a second ago, he knew it had to be there, it was in a perfect line from the one to the east. He spun his body around and looked back to make sure he hadn't somehow moved from his usual straight line and swum diagonally outwards. He hadn't. The buoys were set in a line each year from May through to October. They ran from Shoreham in the west all the way along the seafront to Brighton Marina in the east, split only by the Palace Pier, with one left on both sides of the pier in a straight line to warn boats not to get too close. But they were all now gone. He twisted around again and looked west to the West Pier. But the burnt-out husk was gone, and in its place was a half-built pier jutting out into the sea.

Breathing heavily, he turned his gaze to the seafront in front of the West Pier, fearful of what he might see, or more to the point of what he would not see. The i360 had disappeared. The tallest, thinnest structure in the world had vanished in the time it had taken him to swim under the pier from one beach to the next. His head swam in confusion. He spun back to focus on the Palace Pier, but it too was gone, replaced further down by an older pier made of chains. And beyond that there was nothing, just sea. Even the monolithic outline of the marina was no longer there in the far distance.

Panic overtook him. He gasped for breath as he struggled to stay afloat, the ability to stay on top of the water suddenly taken from him as his mind refused to grasp what his eyes were showing him. He sank beneath the water, his mouth stuck open, letting sea water pour in, forcing the air from his lungs as he started to drown. Suddenly from nowhere, almost slicing his head in two, a rowboat came flying past, its oar so close he could feel the pressure leave it as the arm inside the boat heaved it forward, cutting through the water like butter. He forced his mind to take hold of his body once more and pushed his feet down as hard as he could, raising himself back up to the surface, coughing up the salty water as he broke free. Getting air back into his lungs, he tried calling to the rower for help. But whoever it was didn't hear him and carried on heading straight to the shore. The beach was so full of people that it was almost impossible to see the stones under their picnic blankets. A beach that a few minutes ago was completely devoid of life.

In front of the boat was a lone swimmer: a man. The boat caught up to him and the oarsman leaned over and shouted something. Even in his panicked, disbelieving state, Jesse could see it was a lady in the rowboat shouting out commands. Her strawberry blonde hair blew around her head as the wind from the sea took hold of it, and her pixie-shaped face was so white it was almost translucent. Jesse watched the exchange between the two, knowing he was gazing at a private and secret moment.

Without warning, the lady turned around and saw him spying on them, intruding on their affair. Her features turned in an instant from joy to hatred. Her deep blue eyes burnt into him, willing him to leave them alone, desperate for more time to finish whatever it was she needed to do.

Despite the look of hatred that she sent him, Jesse felt compelled to be with her, to touch her; he wanted to be next to her in the boat and pull her in close to him. The swimmer kept going, heading to the beach. The woman tore her eyes away from Jesse and thrust the two oars deep into the water and followed the swimmer to the beach. Desperate not to lose her, Jesse forced his head and shoulders back down into the sea and swam harder than he had ever swum before, all thoughts of nearly drowning already forgotten. All the years of swimming in pools as a child, of studying the greats to learn how they could move so effortlessly through the water kicked in. He reached the sea edge in under a minute, his feet finding the seabed quicker than he expected. He looked up for the boat and the girl; but they were gone.

They should have been right where he stood. He had followed her wake; he had felt the thrust of the water as she dragged the boat forward and had felt himself close in on her with every pull of his arms. He swung his head around, desperate to see her, but there was no one. He turned back and faced the beach. It too was completely empty. No crowds, no picnic blankets, nothing but cold, hard pebbles.

He sensed something else, something in his peripheral vision. He slowly and fearfully turned his eyes to the west, and before him, at the edge of the seafront, rising high up into the sky was the i360, its doughnut-shaped pod floating up with the first of the day trippers ready to view the ocean from a hundred and sixty-two metres above sea level. Just beyond stood the burnt-out shell of the West Pier, and to the east, the Palace Pier and then the marina.

The strength left him and he collapsed onto the beach, trembling.

It was about a minute before he came to, lying on the beach trembling from the cold. A small group of people were standing around him, watching, but unable or unsure what they needed to do. He had to draw on all the skills Marlene had taught him to clear his mind and relax his breathing. He lay back on the stones and let himself just be. He thought back to Marlene's often repeated words to him when he was too anxious to relax…

"We are called human *be*ings, Jesse, not human *do*ings. Stop doing and just be…"

All thoughts slowly vanished as he brought himself slowly and calmly back to the present. With the help of the small group that had gathered, he was able to pull himself up to stand on his feet. After a few more seconds, he found he was ready to move once again. Thanking everyone for their help, he slowly staggered back up the beach, having to bend low to walk under the pier and back onto his own side to collect his crocs.

★★★

Once at the arch, Jesse showered and changed, his mind replaying the images of the beautiful girl in the boat, her pale skin and her eyes, light blue and full of mischief, yet seemingly lifeless at the same time.

With no one else coming in after him, he switched off the lights and headed for the door, stopping only to sign out his name in the diary. As he did so, he noticed the blank lines that separated his name from the early morning swimmers. The name with the two letter 'A's was no longer there. Jesse spun around to face the wall behind him and hanging in the spot where it always had was the photo of Adam Austin, James, Alex, Mike and Little Bob, the last photo ever taken of them all together before Adam died. Jesse stared at it, tying to understand what he had just witnessed out on the beach. The picture showed the friends standing in the sea next to the Palace Pier during a low tide, perhaps just half a metre in depth, the small waves lapping at their ankles. All of them wearing the orange BSC swim caps, their goggles up on their heads like sunglasses ready for a sunny day, and relaxed smiles fixed to their faces showing the obvious joy they had at being in the cold sea on a weekday morning before work. Jesse stood and looked at it for a few minutes, his eyes fixing on those of Adam Austin. He now knew who he had seen swimming around the buoy and under the pier just now.

"That was you, Adam, wasn't it? Did you take me under the pier so you could show me Lilly?" Jesse asked the picture. "Who is she then, and who was she following in her boat? Did you follow her in her rowing boat as well? Is that what happened? Did she pull you into that storm? I don't know why, but I think she's back, and I think it's you bringing me here, to this club. What do you want with me, Adam?" he asked out loud into the arch.

There was no reply, the arch and Jesse's mind remained silent.

He walked away from the picture before pressing the green button on the wall next to the door commanding it to swing open. As he left, he realised that the temperature in the arch once again matched the warm temperature out on the seafront. He shivered despite the warmth.

The shutter closed behind him as he swiped his fob on the sensor, and, leaving the arch behind, he walked down the beach to check everything was where it should be – that the pier hadn't somehow vanished again while he had grabbed a quick shower.

The yellow buoys were all still there in a straight line from the marina, through to the Palace Pier and under the silver ball to the west. And the i360 was once again heading up its tower with a new group of tourists in its gleaming glass pod.

CHAPTER EIGHT

Natalie

High above the seafront, oblivious of the man a mile away on the beach gazing up at the i360 pod she was in, Natalie stood with her friend. As the pod reached its final destination, Natalie leaned into the glass and gazed out at the view. The sea was as calm as a millpond and the seagulls floated in the air as if they were puppets on an invisible string.

"Are you OK, Nat?" Sharon asked her.

"I guess so."

"I really don't know why you put yourself through this. It must be so hard for you, coming here, to the seafront, what with..." she trailed off.

"It was at first," Natalie said. "But actually, it somehow makes me feel close to him again. I bet you didn't know that I've been up here every week since it opened. It's funny, really, as I never thought I'd want to, but I just need to face the sea every day and this seemed the easiest way, close but safe behind the glass. I think I'm kind of hooked now."

"And the kids?" Sharon said, staring over to the other side of the pod where Daisy and Alfie were sitting on the floor chatting away.

Natalie wasn't sure exactly what to tell her friend. Natalie used to tell Sharon everything, but of late she had become even more withdrawn.

"What's happening, Nat? You and the twins seem to have more space between you now than you ever have."

"We don't seem to be much of a family any more. They've just kind of cut me out completely, everything is a whisper and a secret. It's like it's them against everyone else, even me."

Opening up to her friend was like a release. For the next ten minutes, as the pod descended back to earth, Natalie spoke at a hundred miles an hour, telling Sharon all about the twins no longer sharing anything with her, how they were always huddled into corners and how recently Daisy had been having bad nightmares, but was refusing to tell her about them.

"Have you spoken to the school to see what they are like there?" Sharon asked.

"I guess I should. But I've been scared to, in case they tell me everything's normal."

"What do you mean?" Sharon asked.

"Well, if it's normal at school, if they are doing well and no one is concerned about them, then I'll know it's only me they won't talk to. I'm not sure I could handle that."

The pod glided to a stop and the doors opened. The twins left and went and sat down on the beach. Natalie and Sharon walked over and sat on a bench opposite and watched them play, not saying anything more to each other, just watching the tide ebb and flow.

CHAPTER NINE

Marlene

"So, you think it was the spirit of Adam Austin you saw in the sea and that he somehow took you back to Lilly's time?"

"It sounds mad, but I don't know what else to think."

Jesse got up, walked into the kitchen and poured himself a glass of water. Marlene carried on talking.

"If you're right, then it means you were able to connect with Adam in one time period – what, five years ago? – and then be taken back to Lilly's time, which you would guess is when? Around the mid-1800s. That's amazing, Jesse, being able to go back to two different time spots in one go. And you're sure it was her again in the boat? And who was it she was following?"

"I don't know who she was following, perhaps it was the man she works for, the one she's having the affair with? It was definitely Lilly in the boat, and I can tell you that she was as shocked to see me as I was her."

"So, we know it wasn't her who dragged you back there then?"

"I guess not."

"OK, so we think that for some reason Adam took you back to witness something between Lilly and someone. What we need to find out is who and why. What connects them all? How did they know each other? We already know that Adam drowned, but what happed to Lilly, and when? When did she die? Certainly before Adam, a long time before."

"The time was all mixed up. One minute I was standing on the beach watching Adam Austin swimming around a buoy, and he died what, five years ago, then as soon as I swam under the pier, I was sometime in the 1800s."

Jesse leaned back in the chair, trying to remember everything he saw. "Go on," she prompted.

"The people on the beach were dressed differently. The women were wearing fancy clothes, long dresses neck to feet, and the men were in dapper suits topped off with hat and cane, even the men heading to the water were dressed in some kind of all-in-one long johns. Absolutely nothing like we wear today. And the West Pier was still under construction, it had hardly left the seafront and, of course, there was no Palace Pier, or Brighton Marina. And Adam, he was in a swimming club cap when I saw him in the sea; none of it fitted together."

"So what does your instinct tell you?" she prompted again, leaning forward now, desperately trying to help him focus.

"For Adam, it was 2012 when he left the arch and swam under the pier. I was watching him in 2012. But then, when he went under the pier, he was in Lilly's time. Somehow she had taken him back to her own time, when she was a young lady, and he was showing me that. I just don't know why Lilly would take Adam back there, or why Adam would show me."

"So we know Lilly lived in the mid-1800s?" Marlene tried to keep Jesse on the dates.

Jesse leaned forward, his eyes closed, thinking back to what he had seen, drawing in as much as he could from just a few hours before.

"I'm not a historian, but it must be around then as that's when the West Pier was just being built."

He slumped back in his chair, exhausted.

"Well done, Jesse," Marlene said, the kindness in her voice replacing the urgency that she had inflicted on him a moment ago. "I know it's exhausting recalling things in such detail. I'll get you some tea and then you can sleep it off. I need you energised for tomorrow." Jesse looked up at her enquiringly. "Tomorrow, it's time for us to do some digging."

"Digging?" Jesse asked with trepidation.

"Not actual digging," she said with a smile. "We're not gravediggers, Jesse. Well, perhaps we are, maybe we are metaphorical gravediggers. Tomorrow I'm going to the library; it's time for me to take a visit to the 1800s."

"And me?" Jesse asked with concern.

"I need you to find out all you can about Adam. If you're right, then something brought Lilly back for Adam Austin, and now she's back again; but for who, we don't know. For you, or maybe for the girl in your dreams, or for someone else? We need to know everything we can about them all. If Lilly came back for Adam, and if you're right, then she may well have been the reason he drowned. So why is she back? Who does she want now? And how is the girl in your dreams mixed up in all this?"

"Hold it right there, Miss Marple, this isn't a game. Lilly's as real as you or me. And I think she's dangerous."

"I'm not proposing a game, Jesse. And she's not real in the sense we are, she's a spirit and I doubt she can physically hurt us."

"You doubt? That's not good enough for me."

"It's all we've got. But if she did lure Adam to his death then she's capable of doing the same to you. We need to stop her before she gets further into your head like she might've done to him."

"And how the hell do we stop a bloody ghost, Marlene?"

"You're the ghost hunter, Jesse, you tell me."

"I'm not a bloody ghost hunter!" he snapped, frustrated.

"Then we really are in trouble," she replied before walking back into the kitchen and switching the kettle on.

CHAPTER TEN

Marlene

Marlene stood on Euston Road London and stared up at the entrance to the British Library. Part of her wanted to turn around and run. She hadn't been back since she had stolen the ghost hunter papers and there was a part of her that expected a guard to run out at any moment and grab her.

As it turned out, the welcome she received was much more cordial. "Welcome back, madam. It's been a while," the familiar security guard said as he pulled open the large doors for her.

"It has," she replied. "You have a good memory. I've missed this place," she said looking around her. "I just love the smell of books; it takes me right back to my childhood. A time before eBooks," she said wistfully, longing for a time when computers didn't rule the world.

"It certainly does, madam," he replied with a nod.

"Excuse me, where are the toilets?" a voice interrupted their conversation.

"By the lift," he barked aggressively at the student. "Sorry, madam, you were saying?"

"Just that I love the smell of old books," Marlene replied, desperate to escape him before he became suspicious of her jittery demeanour.

"So do I, madam," he said, sucking in the air through his

nostrils as he smiled and moved aside so that she could enter the grand hall.

She shuffled past him, wiping away the bead of sweat running down the right side of her face with her right hand, her left clutching nervously at her shoulder bag. She had no intention of stealing another book from here, or in fact of ever stealing anything again from anywhere. However, on leaving her house that morning, she had subconsciously found herself taking hold of the old shoulder bag that she used to carry around university over forty years ago. It could hold any number of things in any number of its secret little pouches, and while she knew she could never do it again, there was a part of her that desperately wanted to be led to another secret treasure, and she didn't want to risk having nothing to hide it in.

Marlene loved this building and knew every inch of it. Standing in the vast entrance hall, she looked up and could see floor after floor winding upwards into the heavens. She had once read that when it had been constructed, the building was the largest of its type in the United Kingdom. It was set over fourteen floors, nine above ground, five below, and it covered over a hundred thousand square metres. Its job was to preserve and protect well over a hundred and fifty million items, with over three million added every year.

Manuscripts, maps, newspapers, magazines, prints, drawings, music scores, patents and, of course, books. The building was a virtual prison of stories and facts. It always saddened her to think that somewhere in here were stories that may never again be read, lessons that may never again be taught and secrets that had never been shared since even before they had been committed to paper. And somewhere in here could be a word or a paragraph that could be the start of the yellow brick road that would eventually lead her and Jesse to Lilly. Throughout its vast chambers, the British Library stored information on every birth and death in England since its records first began. All she had to do was start narrowing it down: decade, place, first name and hopefully surname. The first step was to head to the eighth floor where the computer desks could be found.

From its opening at ten in the morning to its closure at six at night, seven days a week, over sixteen thousand people would walk its corridors daily, and today was no exception. The eighth floor was always particularly busy; such was the power of the internet. Without the search engine that was built to reference all the articles within, it would take over eighty thousand years to get through the whole collection; something Marlene certainly did not have time for!

In the old days of her research, Marlene would have found the longest-serving member of staff and quizzed them endlessly, teasing out the knowledge they stored in their heads about each floor, each shelf and those special areas that the general public were not allowed access to. But with the advent of computer referencing, the librarian had quickly become an expensive commodity that the library could ill afford and they had been replaced with high-tech, superfast broadband and part-time students to simply ensure books were put back where they should be and copies were scanned into the system.

It was nearly an hour before Marlene could secure her position in front of one of the computers and she had spent that time hovering anxiously behind a late-stage scholar, while reading and rereading all her notes from her last session with Jesse.

By the time she pulled up the library schematic on the screen, she had already decided on her levels of attack:

1. Name – Lilly *something*.
2. The surname Austin.
3. Brighton seafront.
4. Time – between the mid-1800s to mid-1900s.
5. Age – mid to late-twenties.

It was very little to go on, but it was a start, and every journey had to begin somewhere.

The initial searches brought up nothing. She shoved the keyboard back in frustration and sat staring at the screen, mumbling obscenities under her breath, pleased the computer couldn't answer her back. She recognised she needed help. She'd already been there for over an hour trying to look up old records and hadn't found much that seemed to be of any help. The only thing she found vaguely interesting and possibly related was a reference to a storm that had ravaged the old Chain Pier and involved a hotel called the Austin Hotel on the Brighton seafront in the mid-1800s.

The old newspaper story described the worst storm recorded in over a hundred years that partly destroyed the Chain Pier off the seafront in Brighton. Guests from the various lodging houses on the seafront had gone out in the great storm to offer help to those stranded, but what really stood out for her was the specific mention of staff and management from a hotel, the Austin Hotel, giving out blankets to those who had been on the pier when it happened and the story of a young lady who had fallen into the sea from the landing platform and been washed away. The victim, whose identity was unknown, was thought to have worked in one of the hotels…

The article was so old and had been scanned in so badly that Marlene could barely make out the words, and the paper ended with a tear at the bottom corner obscuring the rest. There was a pencil sketch attached depicting a hotel. From her knowledge of Brighton's seafront, she thought she recognised it as the place where the Queens Hotel now stood, but maybe, she thought, over a hundred years ago it was called something else, maybe there was even an Austin Hotel on that site back then. Either way, it was of no immediate help; she was looking for a girl called Lilly in her twenties who had lived and perhaps died in Brighton, she was not searching for a hotel.

"Can I help you?" the lady behind the counter said, after keeping Marlene waiting for more than fifteen minutes while she slowly finished directing a group of students to the modern literature section.

"Is there anyone who can help me on the archive computer, please?"

"Isn't it working? I'm sure it was fine the last time it was used. I'll call maintenance," the lady said, picking up the phone and turning around to find the number from her index box.

"It's working fine, I just need some help searching for someone," Marlene said a little desperately.

"Maintenance, it's Ruby up on research eleven. Apparently, the archives aren't working again."

"Excuse me, I just need some help," Marlene tried again.

"Yes, I can hold."

Ruby seemed oblivious to Marlene as she held the phone to her ear and went back to her filing.

"For goodness' sake!" Marlene said as she turned back around looking to see if there was anyone else who could help her.

"Anything I can do for you?"

A young man came out from a side door near the desk having heard Marlene's frustrated voice.

"I need help doing some research and was hoping that lady would help me."

"Ruby!" The boy laughed. "She's not really the computer kind. I'm Simon, I'm doing some volunteer work here. What do you need? Maybe I can help."

"I'm trying to find some information on someone who I think lived in Brighton years ago, someone who maybe was murdered or died in a mysterious way."

"Brighton, I love it. A great place; I graduated from the university there."

"So, do you think you can help?" she asked him.

"I'd imagine so. How long ago are we talking about?"

"I'm not entirely sure. I've an approximate time of around mid-1800s, the names are Austin and Lilly, but not a lot more. I started looking myself but only found one article and I'm not sure it's that helpful; it did mention the name Austin, but not in the way I was expecting."

"It's a start. Show me what you found."

Leaving Ruby hanging on the phone, Marlene led Simon back into the archive room and let him sit in front of the computer she'd been using while she pulled up a chair next to him.

"So," he said, as his fingers went naturally to the keyboard. "You're in 1864 by the looks of things. A storm that destroyed the pier. OK, so tell me what it is you're after exactly."

His fingers flew across the keyboard as Marlene explained to him everything she knew so far, which was pretty much limited to the names Lilly someone and Austin.

After watching pages flash by for the better part of forty minutes, Simon sat back in his chair with a satisfied look on his face.

"I couldn't find anything in Brighton that specifically referenced a girl called Lilly, so I extended the search to villages and towns in the area. Again, nothing came up, so I extended the search to London. I figured maybe she was born in London and travelled to Brighton, a lot of people did that back then; still do, I reckon," he said with a smile.

"And?" Marlene prompted him.

"Well, Lilly was not a popular name back then and so while there are a few references to the name, there was a girl in London who caused a bit of a stir. A young girl called Lilly Baker went missing after a murder back in 1851; it says here that she might have been one of the youngest known murderers in London at the time. It looks like they never found her."

"Go on."

Marlene felt a flicker of butterflies in her stomach. Could this be the start? Could this Lilly Baker from London really be Jesse's mysterious Lilly from Brighton? It seemed a long shot, but maybe it was the first step in tracking down Jesse's ghost.

"There's not a great deal about it. There was a workhouse, an orphanage by today's name, I guess. Although back then, workhouses were for the unloved and unwanted; terrifying places. This was one of the oldest in London, opened in 1697, actually, on Rose Street, London, called St Anne's. Back in 1851, a girl vanished after a priest was murdered; a young girl about thirteen years old called Lilly Baker. It doesn't say much more; only that she was the main suspect. It suggests she might have left London and gone on the run."

"Surely a girl running away from one of those places wasn't uncommon?"

Marlene was feeling the frustration again as it seemed this was maybe starting to come to nothing.

"True enough," continued Simon. "But you said *murdered or mysterious death* and this story on Lilly Baker definitely has mystery and murder in it. The article says the girl ran away after murdering the priest who ran the house. Blimey, it says she stabbed him through the throat and let him bleed to death. She was seriously damaged this girl!"

Simon carried on, "There's another article here about it. There was another girl with her at the time, a Melody Parsons. It says that this Melody Parsons swore that Lilly murdered the priest and then calmly walked away leaving her lying on the floor soaked in the blood."

Simon scrolled through a few more pages before looking back up at Marlene.

"Melody was hanged as an accomplice to the murder but they never found Lilly. This article says they thought she might have tried to escape over the River Thames somehow and might have drowned. The Thames was deadly back then, full of shit and stuff. If she went in there she definitely wouldn't have got out. I don't know if it's the same girl you're looking for, but it's the same name and similar time."

"Maybe," Marlene replied.

Simon continued to scroll through more screens but found nothing else. "Nope, I can't find anything else about this Lilly. What about that other name you mentioned, Austin, wasn't it?"

Before Marlene could answer him, Simon's fingers started across the keyboard again.

Excitedly he looked at Marlene.

"There was an Austin Hotel on Brighton seafront." He continued reading.

"Here we go," he said. "There was also a John Austin, the manager and co-owner of the Austin Hotel back in the 1800s."

"John Austin," Marlene said, startled.

She hadn't noticed any specific names when she'd looked before.

"Yes, it looks like it was an old family-run hotel back in the time you're talking about and it was run by a man called John Austin."

"What else does it say?" she asked, her excitement starting to grow.

"It made the headlines when that storm you read about hit. Let me go back a bit further and see what else there is."

Marlene watched as Simon trawled through the archive computer, somehow able to dissect the information in milliseconds and knowing when to pause or flick through to the next screen.

"Ah… this is interesting," he said, leaning back a bit so Marlene could look more closely at the screen. "A few months after the storm, the hotel was sold. The stories are a bit muddled but they talk about the Austin Hotel being sold by the family because of the tragic deaths, plural! It doesn't say who, though, just deaths, so either that's bad writing or there was more than one person who died."

"Two deaths, then." Marlene leaned in closer. "Does it say anywhere who they were?"

"It doesn't name anyone, but further on it references a member of staff who was washed off the Chain Pier and then one of the owners of the hotel dying in the building the same day. But that's it. It's odd that it doesn't say anything else about them, only it jumps forward to later that year and the sale."

"So John Austin sold the hotel. And Adam Austin was clearly related to him, but who died on the pier?" Marlene mused.

"Who's Adam Austin?" Simon asked, suddenly drawn into the saga.

"He was a swimmer who died in Brighton a few years back, apparent suicide."

"A swimmer?" Simon looked confused.

"Adam Austin died in a storm five years ago off Brighton Beach."

"So, if they are related, this Adam Austin and this John Austin, then they are an unlucky family, aren't they?"

"What do you mean?" Marlene was suddenly interested in Simon's theories.

"Well, if they are related as you say, then it seems John Austin was involved somehow in two deaths and then Adam Austin killed himself right on the same seafront. I'm just saying, not a lucky family."

"Is there anything else?" Marlene asked.

Simon's fingers went back to the keyboard and words and documents scrolled once again across the screen. Marlene sat back, happy to let the young man do his thing, grateful at last to feel that she was doing something practical to help Jesse. And she could see by his enthusiasm that he was enjoying helping her as much as she needed him to.

"I'm so grateful for your help, Simon, you really are saving me days, if not weeks of research."

"It's a pleasure; if I'm honest, I wish I had more projects like this to work on," he replied without taking his eyes off the screen. Simon spent thirty minutes searching more about the Austin Hotel, but there was little he could find that they didn't already know.

"Let's look further afield," Simon suggested. "Let's see if we can tie my Lilly Baker to your Lilly and establish if she came to Brighton. I studied the history of Brighton during my course at Sussex Uni – the people and the places. It was a completely different landscape from how it is now, it was all farmland around the Lanes back then, and the seafront was mostly fishermen and sea trade and some small lodging houses. People came from all over, drawn out of the big cities by the clean sea air. There were too many of them to be recorded; maybe Lilly Baker was one of them. Maybe she came to Brighton from London after she murdered that priest and no one ever knew?" The library archives were little help in the wider search, so Simon switched to the internet. Without a break, he pressed harder, digging and digging, pulling up as many references as he could. The only other article he found that had any reference to Lilly Baker told in more detail the story of the gruesome murder they had uncovered earlier in their search. The article continued, two girls had committed the atrocity; one of them named as Lilly Baker, the other was held at the scene covered in blood and confessing. After the hanging of Melody, a limited search was made of the city, but the missing child was never apprehended.

Marlene sat back in her chair, her eyes strained from reading for so many hours, suddenly convinced that she had found *her* Lilly Baker.

"What do you think?" asked Simon. "Have I found your Lilly?"

"I think you might have done. If I was to make an educated

guess, I'd say she killed that priest and then ran away to Brighton. Maybe she ended up at the Austin Hotel somehow, maybe she was given a job there; it's perhaps tenuous but it certainly ties her to John Austin and in turn links her to Adam. You've been a great help, Simon, thank you."

"My pleasure. It's been fun."

"You must let me give you something for your time. It feels like I've taken up your whole day."

"It's cool, I enjoyed it. I don't normally get to do this mystery stuff."

Marlene gathered her bag together and headed out of the library, relieved at having some information to take away with her; she was certain she now knew Lilly's surname and she could, using a little artistic licence, tie her into the Austin family first through John and then to Adam Austin.

The sun outside was setting as the streetlights came on and burnt into the darkness left behind. She walked down the main steps, heading to King's Cross station, just ten minutes' walk away, to get the Tube back to Victoria Station and then the train back to Hassocks, the closest station to her house in Hurstpierpoint. She was desperate to update Jesse on what she had found out.

She dialled Jesse's number.

"Please leave a message and I'll call you back," came the reply.

"Jesse, it's me. Where are you? Did you find out anything about Adam Austin? I've been doing some research and I've got some stuff you should know about Lilly and an Austin Hotel and its owner John Austin. Her surname's Baker, Lilly Baker. I am sure it's the same girl. If what I've found is right, you've been pulled into something that you shouldn't be. And I've still no idea who the girl in your dream is, but if she's related to Adam then we should try to find out. Can you call me please as soon as you've got this message?"

The phone beeped, ending the message before she was finished.

Frustrated, she dialled a second number. The phone rang seven times before it was answered by a high-pitched voice just as Marlene was about to cut off.

"Hello, hello, who is it?" The voice had a strong Italian accent, and was distorted by an echo, as if it was being spoken from a large empty building.

"Sofia, it's Marlene."

"Marlene, darling, how lovely, been too long. How are you? Still chasing spirits around the room? Ha."

"I haven't got long, I've a train to get," she said, interrupting her friend. "Are you in the UK at the moment? I might need your help."

"Oh no, so sorry, I'm away. I'm just in the airport at Rome and jumping on a plane to Norway. I'm speaking at a convention this week. What you do need, sweetheart?"

"I've been doing some research on someone and I think I've found something, but really I need an expert now."

"Ha. Sofia is the expert for sure, yes. You want to email and I'll look."

"I'd rather see you in person if I can. When are you back?"

"Week maybe, not more. Come visit, yes? We'll catch up. I'll help you. Yes, good yes. Call in about a week, good, bye, bye, bye, bye, bye."

Sofia always finished with a machine gun farewell before ending her calls.

The phone went dead. Marlene wished she'd called her friend before. Sofia was one of the top genealogists in the world and maybe she could find something in the Austin family tree that could provide them with more answers. She put the phone back in her bag, making a mental note to call Sofia in a week's time, and headed down into the underground station.

As she walked down the steps, her stomach lurched. It was a feeling she'd had many times before. Usually it presaged the arrival of a message from the spirit world, but today, as she descended into the darkness, an unexpected fear started to overwhelm her. Looking around, it occurred to her that the lights were too dim down there and, unusually, there was no one else about; no one at all, not even at the barriers or the sales desk. She spun around, her ears drawn to a noise, but there was nothing there. She jumped as a shadow crossed her vision, but again there was nothing.

"Pull yourself together, lady," she told herself, speaking out loud to break the silence. "Where is everyone?" she continued talking to herself. "Which line did I come in on?" All the colours on the Tube map suddenly looked the same, the lines indistinguishable from each other. With the sound of her heart thundering in her ears, Marlene quickened her pace, desperate to find some people. Every instinct within her was screaming for her to turn back. But she couldn't. It was as if an invisible force was pushing her forward. She stepped onto the escalator. Her eyes were suddenly very itchy, her head thumped with the beginnings of a migraine and her chest felt tight. She wanted to turn around, but movement was impossible.

From nowhere, a strange perfume ran down her throat. She coughed violently, bending over slightly at the waist, feeling herself unbalance. Straightening, she shivered. There was someone behind her. She turned slowly, cursing herself for carrying on into the station. She'd confronted spirits before, so why did she feel so powerless now?

As her head came around, the temperature dropped from a stifling thirty degrees to a chilling zero. But still there was no one there. She hugged herself as the chill seeped through her clothes. She turned back around and her blood froze. A girl with strawberry blonde hair and lifeless blue eyes was standing on the step directly in front of her. Crying out, Marlene reached out to her instinctively, and then she was falling forwards, her hands going straight through the girl as if she weren't there.

She fell headfirst down the last ten metres, the escalator tearing at the skin on her face as she rolled over and over until she settled at the bottom. The last thing Marlene saw before everything went black was the darkness in the girl's eyes, and she knew then that she was staring into the eyes of Lilly Baker.

CHAPTER ELEVEN

Jesse

J esse wasn't sure where to begin.

When Marlene had suggested she researched Lilly while he found out about Adam, he was at first relieved. Lilly scared him. It wasn't just that she was a ghost, he'd been aware of ghosts as long as he could remember. And it wasn't the usual feeling of unease that he'd feel just before he'd see a spirit. It went way beyond that. Lilly was something else, something much more. He'd felt it in the arch before he'd gone into the sea the previous morning, that feeling of cold, and the severe pain in the pit of his stomach. He'd also felt it when he'd looked into her eyes from under the pier. And then he'd felt it again when she was trying to draw the child into her nightmare and push him away; he knew now that it had been Lilly all along. She did not want him to see this, or feel this, she was pushing him away while she was drawing the young child in.

He'd never felt so intensely conflicted before – he needed to know more and to try to protect this unknown child, but at the same time he wanted to run away and have nothing to do with it. If it were not for Marlene taking control, he knew he would have locked his flat up and run away weeks ago. It was what he always did when things became too much for him. But he couldn't leave; not now. Not when Marlene had set him on a course. He had to see it through. Also, if he left now, then he would be leaving

78

Marlene; the only person in the world who could show him how to reach deeply into the spirit world and find his family. This had been his purpose since he first agreed to see her and he was not yet ready to give that up. She was too precious to him for too many reasons to abandon her now. That above all would keep him coming back again and again even when all his instincts screamed at him to run away and never look back.

There had to be a link between Lilly, the child in his dreams and Adam Austin. And Adam was currently the easiest lead he could follow.

So far, all he knew was what he had learned from members of the swimming club, that Adam had been a strong swimmer, was happily married to a girl called Natalie and had been the proud father of twins: a girl and a boy, Alfie and Daisy. He also knew that he had been a popular member of the swimming club and by all accounts had been a success in business and most probably in life. So why had he run into a deadly sea when he would have known better?

Someone had to know something, he just needed to work out who.

An hour later, he had formed a plan. He knew who he needed to speak with, and exactly where to find her. Having managed to get a copy of the swimming club's membership listing all the names, phone numbers and addresses of club members past and existing in the cupboard at the arch, Jesse was now standing nervously outside the gates to Natalie Austin's house.

He stared up at what was a grand house by anyone's standards. Contemporary in design and gleaming in the morning sun. It stood behind big black gates, proudly rising up to four floors. Its entrance hall was a tower of glass encompassing a beautiful chandelier looking out over the road ahead. The driveway was big enough for six cars, but currently held just the one. Lined with beautiful flowers, it delivered you to the foot of a sweeping staircase that could have come straight out of an old Hollywood movie leading up to a large, modern front door. Despite its size and fantastic location off Dyke Road, one of the most expensive roads in Hove, the house somehow retained a feeling of being a family home. Staring up at it, Jesse felt a sense of close family and love. There was something else, though, something that was creeping into his senses as he continued to gaze at the grand staircase through the closed gates. A feeling of loss and fear. The house and its occupants had lost something important, something that all the grandeur could never replace.

Jesse pressed the buzzer at the entrance panel on the gate and waited, secretly hoping that no one would answer so he could just turn away and tell Marlene that he had tried his best. There was no reply from the speaker apart from a slight buzz, and Jesse felt his shoulders start to relax just a little. Maybe there was no one home; it seemed like he had been saved an intrusive and difficult conversation. As he turned to walk over to his bike chained to a fence a few metres down, he felt the sudden instinct that someone was staring at him. He turned back.

His gaze settled on the large picture window that stood above the front door. Two small faces stared out at him. One of them held his gaze. Jesse gasped in shock. He had never seen her before but he knew exactly who she was. They had shared several moments together; moments of fear when he had used all his strength to protect her. Their eyes locked for a moment, then, in a flash, she turned and ran away from the window further into the house, the other child following her close behind.

Jesse stood, frozen with shock, staring at the place where the children had been. He wasn't sure whether he should ring the buzzer again, or just leave. He was brought back to his senses by the creeping sensation that someone else was looking at him. He glanced around. No one was there. But he could feel a presence, something cold and menacing. He closed his eyes and dug deep within himself, as Marlene had taught him, trying to understand where this feeling was coming from. Terror overwhelmed him as he felt a dark malice emanating towards him. He dug down further still, keeping Marlene's words in his head, forcing his fear aside, trying to pull whatever it was even closer to him. But it was too strong. The more he tried to pull it in, the further it pushed him away.

"Orange," he whispered to himself.

His throat tightened as the faint smell of burnt orange seeped into his lungs. He wanted to cough it away, but instead he held it in, took it deep into his lungs like smoke from a cigarette. He knew that, whatever it was, it was important, and he needed to keep it close, to taste it and to understand it. But it went as quickly as it had come. Released from his trance, he realised the sky was darkening and getting stormy, and even as he ran back to his bike, the first thick drops of rain started to fall down on him. He sped down the road, his wheels skidding under him as he pushed his legs faster and faster, heading straight into a storm of his own.

★★★

Natalie swept open the front door to find the street below empty. Through the rain, she could see a man climbing onto a bike, but she didn't recognise him. A sudden waft of burnt orange held her in place. She coughed as it caught in her throat, bringing with it a difficult memory. She'd smelled this scent before. The day she'd watched Adam walk out of the door for the last time. The morning of his death. Adam had often complained about that smell, at first questioning where it came from, but eventually calling it *her* perfume.

As it crept down her throat, it sickened her.

The smell and taste evaporated as quickly as they had come, leaving her feeling weak and nervous. She stood at the front door

81

for a few minutes more and watched as the unknown cyclist headed down the road through the sudden rainstorm.

★★★

As if on autopilot, Jesse reached the arch in record time, despite the weather, and chained his bike to the railings on the seafront. He pulled the rucksack off his back, not even questioning why he had taken his swimming bag with him to Adam's house in the first place, and walked down to the arch.

Leaving his bag on his usual corner bench, he changed, turned off the lights and lowered the shutters, leaving the arch sealed and undisturbed.

Walking down the beach, he felt mildly surprised that he couldn't feel the pebbles biting into his feet, nor, though he was aware of it, could he feel the rain pouring down on him. He noticed, with mild interest, that the wind was whipping his hair around wildly, and the sea was heading for a high tide, pitching rolling waves fiercely at the shore. But he didn't care. He kept on walking to the water's edge where, without pausing, he dived straight into a terrifyingly heavy wave.

CHAPTER TWELVE

James

For normal people, today was not a day to be at the beach. The sea had worked herself up into a bad mood since James had arrived on the shore, and she was extremely angry. The flags on the pier were flapping so hard that they were just a blur of colour, and the water was being churned into a maelstrom. Far out at sea, the waves were huge; roller-coaster waves you'd want to avoid unless you were intent on dying. James knew that if they were lucky enough to make it into the sea alive, they certainly didn't want to be unlucky enough to be caught up in the waves on the return journey to shore. Waves that size could break bones as if they were twigs. At the shore, they were just as murderous. It was one thing to battle the waves and be spun around as if on a fairground ride, but it was quite another to then try to land *safely* and in one piece back on the land.

Their beach adjacent to Palace Pier had a shelf near the shore that curled under at an extreme pitch, so if one of those waves grabbed a swimmer as they were trying to get in or out, it could literally spin them under and drag them across the seabed like a toy in a washing machine. It could happen in the shallowest areas off the shelf. Even the strongest swimmers at the Brighton Sea Swimming Club were no match for a wave that was out to get them.

James reached the arch just before 10am and as expected on a morning like this, he found the shutter closed and the lights off. On a Saturday, they always met at 10am rather than the usual 7am so they could enjoy a more leisurely swim. This morning, though, the swim would be anything but leisurely. By 10:15am, James had been joined by Geoff, Mike and Little Bob, his buddies who never missed a day, no matter the weather. Everyone else had clearly taken the more sensible view of enjoying a morning staying dry and safe. Without much expectation of a swim, they still left the arch in their trunks and headed down to the edge of the sea. They stood at the water's edge for a good two minutes watching the madness as it unfolded.

"I told you, there's no way we can get in there," James said to the others as they edged themselves a little further back from the crashing waves.

As he spoke, a huge wave curled no more than half a metre away and sent pebble gunshot and stinging saltwater straight at them, forcing them to make a sharp retreat. Mike caught a hail of stones in the back of the legs as he ran, causing small cuts all the way up to his thighs.

"Fuck!" he screamed as the sniper wave drew little spots of blood around his calves.

"I'm definitely going in," Geoff shouted above the noise of the wind. They stopped running and he headed back to the edge for another go. "They're in threes, aren't they?" he said, trying to convince the others.

"See, one… two… three…"

Despite the shouts from the others, he still went for it.

But this was the sea they were playing with, not some wave machine in a leisure complex, and the behaviour of waves in the real world can't be predicted. So, despite the sea pulling out and seemingly getting ready to repeat its three waves, break, three waves, break sequence, it instead came charging straight back at Geoff for wave number four. But it was too late for him to turn back. Geoff had already run into what should have been a safe break in the waves. Instead, in a split second, he went from ankle-deep in a receding sea to being dragged under in a swirling mess, his head striking the sea floor violently, his goggles being forced into his eyes and his nose dragged across sunken stone, before he was tossed unceremoniously back onto the beach; bruised, scratched, but thankfully alive.

"I think it's just a groin shower or a pilchard this morning, boys," Little Bob said with a laugh as he, Mike and James helped an unsteady Geoff back to his feet.

"I'll go check the groin to see if the waves are coming over then," James said, walking along the beach closer to the pier to get a look at the large barrier groin to the right of it that jutted out into the sea.

He was back in under a minute and joined the others at the water's edge, the sea forcing them back once again as another wave grabbed handfuls of stones to fire at them.

"Any good?" asked Geoff, as he rubbed his head with frozen fingers, trying to find any broken skin or stones imbedded in him.

"Maybe," James replied. "A couple broke over the edge, but most are hitting the base and just sending spray over. It's pretty hit and miss, I think, hardly what I'd call a shower."

"It's just a pilchard then, I think," Little Bob said, getting ready to lie down on the ground.

"I'd go back a bit," Mike said, lying down a few feet further up the beach. "These waves could drag us right in. It's not worth the risk."

Agreeing with him, the three of them lay down next to Mike, four grown men lying in a line, like pilchards from a tin, childish grins plastered over their faces waiting for the sea to rush over them.

"Here it comes!" James screamed in pleasure, as a monster wave crashed onto the shore and raced up the beach towards them, covering them instantly, washing over them and forcing pebbles up their trunks, seaweed to wrap around their bodies and causing them to crash and roll into each other before it retreated, and in a last gasp attempt, it reached out its claws and tried to drag them back as it raced out ready for the next onslaught.

Digging their fingertips deep into the Brighton pebbles, they resisted the pull-back and quickly reformed their line like knights in a tourney, ready for the next strike.

Five waves and some serious pebble-dashing later, they heaved themselves up and, grinning, fought their way through the wind back up the beach to the safety of the arch.

Geoff continued to examine his head for blood and bruising as they walked back.

"I think I was lucky today, boys," Geoff chirped, trying to draw the others into a conversation about his braveness.

"Stupid, more like," James replied, not wanting to encourage him further. It only took them about thirty seconds to reach the door, but it was another thirty seconds before Little Bob's hands had stopped shaking enough to undo the fob from the thread in his trunks and spring it open. Fortunately, with just four of them, it meant little queuing time for the shower. As soon as they were all showered, dressed and sufficiently warmed up, Geoff's conversation turned from the extreme weather to how brave he had been to even have attempted it today. They all knew glorifying such stupidity when they were together was behaviour worthy of ten-year-olds in the playground, but at just 10:30am on a stormy Saturday morning, that was exactly how they saw themselves; kids playing in an extreme playground.

It was during Geoff's second attempt at describing how his head was forced into the seabed that he first noticed the single bag sitting on the bench in the corner. It was the one thing that could make every single member of the swimming club feel instantly sick. Mid-sentence, he stopped talking, his mouth suddenly as frozen as his fingers had been a moment ago. He looked around at each of them, then back at it, then his gaze turned to the door. Sensing something wasn't right, the others quickly followed his gaze. They'd all experienced this at some time or other. It usually ended very quickly as soon as the door opened and the bag's owner came crashing in, usually with a big grin and swimming trunks, or a bikini full of stones and sand. This time, though, the door didn't crash open.

They knew in the pit of their stomachs that it wasn't going to this time. They had been the only ones there; they would have surely seen someone else coming up the beach if there was anyone else.

They all stared at it – a small Nike sports bag, about thirty inches in length, faded dark blue and stained from day after day of sea salt being left to dry into it. It sat alone without its owner to pick it up and sling it over his shoulder. An ordinary sports bag with the power to make them all feel sick with dread.

"Maybe someone is still out there on the beach; or maybe having a groin shower?" Little Bob said hopefully, interrupting the silence that had suddenly descended on them.

"Was it here before we went out?" Mike asked.

At the arch, they usually noticed bags and clothes. Stuff like that was important. Seeing someone's clothes on a hook or their bag on the bench was like leaving a business card at a networking event. It simply said: "I was here." But this morning, it screamed to them, "I am here, I am still here."

James knew who the bag belonged to. He'd known it was Jesse's the moment he'd followed Geoff's gaze. He had also been there five years before when they had discovered Adam's bag in exactly the same spot, and he'd known it was Adam's straight away that morning as well. That had been a morning like this one, a crazy storm that no one should have been out in, especially not on their own. He felt history starting to repeat itself.

With absolutely no sign of Jesse bursting through the door, James's stomach began to churn.

"It's Jesse's bag," James said, his voice over-loud in the now quiet room. As if a single thought had struck them instantaneously, the four swimmers streaked into action, almost knocking each other over as they rushed out of the narrow doorway and headed back down the beach over the slippery stones. James and Geoff set their eyes to the east of the pier while Mike and Little Bob looked to the west. With such a crazy sea, even standing close to the shore meant the tide was pulling on their shoes and soaking their trousers. It was almost impossible to see anything other than waves darting around like white horses charging down the final furlong – even the seagulls were being beaten back, unable to land on the sea for their morning nap. The waves had picked up to almost twice the size in the few minutes since they had walked back to the arch; the sea could do that, hitting boiling point faster than any kettle. The four of them strained their eyes against the wind, concentrating on trying to spot colours amongst the white, thrashing waves, to see an arm turning over, or an orange swim cap being tossed around. But there was nothing. He wasn't there; or at least he wasn't on top of the sea. "He's in there somewhere, I know he is. ADAM…!" James screamed into the wind.

Mike looked at him as if he had gone mad.

"Adam? Adam's dead, this is Jesse, for God's sake, get a fucking grip, James," Mike screamed back, turning his face away from his friend and back to the sea looking for something, anything that would stand out.

After about five minutes, wind-battered and soaking wet from the sea spray, they headed back to the arch, James's head hanging low, desperate to be wrong about losing another friend. His mind was torn between Adam and Jesse, two friends he realised he could never have saved.

As they walked back, they agreed that maybe the bag had been left there overnight, long before they'd gone down for their earlier swim after all.

"The shutter was down when we got here, wasn't it? The bag was probably there all night," suggested Mike. "We just missed it when we went in, didn't we?"

"Maybe we'll just find some wet trunks and goggles in there. Maybe Jesse had an earlier swim before it got mad out there and then forgot to take the bag home with him," Geoff added.

James didn't believe that for a second. In fact, none of them really believed it, but at a time like this, James was ready to cling on to anything. They all stood staring at the bag again. Geoff stepped forward to pick it up. Being the youngest amongst them by many years, he had less fear of what might lie inside. James already knew what he'd find, he'd been here before. Last time it was him who opened the bag and had found discarded clothes, a letter and a diary. He held his breath as Geoff reached for the zip.

Without any warning, the arch door crashed back on its hinges, the wind forcing an old bamboo fishing rod leaning on the wall to fall into the main room. One of its hooks swung violently past Geoff's face, drawing a line of blood across his cheek. It came to rest on the bag, the hook lodging itself into the fabric.

The four heartbeats flatlined at the same time. In unison, they spun to the doorway, not sure what or who they expected to see standing there. But no one was there.

They stood, staring, immobile, not even breathing, their eyes darting back and forth to each other then back to the door.

Little Bob was the first to speak.

"Fuck me," he said, as he walked to the door and peered out cautiously. He stood at the open arch entrance, looking in all directions, but there was no one out there.

"We couldn't have pulled the door shut," Mike said as he turned back to Geoff. "Go on, open it."

The three others were still in the same position when Bob

turned back into the room and stepped past them to the bag.

"I'll do it," Bob said.

Geoff moved back, his hand covering the gash on his face, pleased to let Bob take the lead. Bob carefully removed the fishing hook from the bag, discarding it into the sink next to him, before pulling the zip back.

The contents were stuffed in without care. Jeans, T-shirt, shoes, socks, boxer shorts; a full day's clothes scrunched up and ready for the washing machine, or the bin – but not a single pair of trunks and no cap or goggles.

Nobody left their clothes there overnight. It confirmed to them what they already knew, that the bag's owner was either still out in the sea or else had had a swim and then walked home in his trunks and hat. Brighton was certainly somewhat eccentric at times, but they silently agreed that a swimming-trunk stroll home in a storm was highly unlikely.

James turned and ran back out of the arch, straight down the beach, his eyes furiously scanning the sea. Geoff, Bob and Mike ran after him, catching him at the edge and pulling him back a second before a wave struck the shore.

"He's out there. I just know he is." James didn't take his eyes off the water.

"If he is, then it's too late. Look out, for Christ's sake," Mike shouted through the wind.

"There!" James shouted to them. "I've got him, by the silver ball, right there!"

All eyes turned in the direction James was suddenly pointing.

"There, look, heading under the pier, an orange swim cap!" He was screaming at them now.

"I don't see anything," Little Bob screamed above the wind. Geoff put his hand on James's shoulder.

"Listen, mate, he isn't there, all right? It wasn't your fault Adam died five years ago and it's not your fault that Jesse went out there today; you couldn't stop him; you weren't even here."

James grabbed Geoff by his head and twisted him violently towards the middle of the pier in the direction of the silver ball that jutted up from the centre of the pier into the sky.

"There!" James screamed. "Look, it's there!"

Geoff concentrated his eyes on the spot and suddenly saw it; an orange speck coming out of the surf, followed by an arm going back under a wave. "Fuck, it's him!" Geoff shouted to them. "Jesse!" Geoff howled into the wind.

"Stay here," James screamed at the three men. "Don't lose him whatever happens; don't let him out of your sight."

He ran back up the beach to the arch and to his phone. He was determined today would not be a repeat of five years ago; he would not lose Jesse like they lost Adam.

CHAPTER THIRTEEN

Marlene

Marlene woke to the sounds of mayhem.

She opened her eyes slowly, afraid. She remembered everything. She had stared into the eyes of death, and now she was terrified about where Lilly might have taken her.

"Take it easy, ma'am." It was an unfamiliar voice, but it was gentle, not the voice she was expecting to hear. "Can you open your eyes for me?" the female voice continued.

Marlene opened her eyes as instructed.

"There you go, see if you can sit up now. Excellent," she said. "I'm Lucinda Graham, head of medical care for the London Underground, she continued as she gently placed a pair of strong hands on Marlene's shoulders and pushed down just hard enough to encourage Marlene to stay still. "You had a fall down the escalator. You've got a few cuts to your face and I think you're likely to get a lump on your head, but I don't think there's any lasting damage. I do need you to stay where you are, though, while I get you checked out by my paramedics, just to be safe."

"Where was everyone?" Marlene asked, half afraid to hear the answer. "What do you mean?" Lucinda asked. "Were you with someone? I was told you were alone."

"I mean everyone else? The whole station was empty, there was no one here. Who found me?"

"Empty?" Lucinda said with a worried expression. "What do you mean?"

"There was no one here, it was so quiet and cold," Marlene whispered.

"It was mobbed, darling, as it always is at this time. You almost knocked a dozen people down the escalator when you fainted. Let me get you some water and let's get you checked out, maybe you have a little concussion after all."

Lucinda heaved her eighteen-stone bulk off the floor with a sigh, squeezed herself out of the small room and headed for the canteen to get some water for Marlene and to chase up the paramedics.

An hour later, having been given the all clear by the overworked paramedics and forced to drink two glasses of iced water, Marlene thanked Lucinda for her help and promised to make sure she stayed hydrated when taking the Tube in future. As her parting gift to Marlene, after making sure her cuts were cleaned and covered, Lucinda had organised a London taxi to take her back to Victoria station. Throughout the taxi ride and for the entire fifty-eight-minute train ride back to Brighton, all Marlene could do was think about what had happened. She tried to convince herself that the paramedics had been right and that after the long session at the library and the searing heat of the Tube station, she was simply overtired and dehydrated and must have passed out. But as much as she wanted to believe that, she knew in her heart that she had seen what she had seen. The underground station had been empty; she was sure of that. And she had tasted something down there; a perfume, which had burnt into her throat making her retch, and something, someone, had made her turn around. And then the cold; she shivered just thinking about it. She knew it was Lilly. She had stared straight into her dead blue eyes. She had got too close to finding out who Lilly was and she had almost paid the price.

In all her years in the job, Marlene had only ever communicated with peaceful spirits. Spirits who had wanted to share their story with her so that she could give comfort to their loved ones. This was her gift and this was the gift she had tried to share and teach to others. Never before had she been touched by evil. And she had only once before, as a young child, actually seen a spirit in form. Back then, it was a middle-aged woman standing over her bed night after night until she had screamed so much that her parents had made her see a doctor who had forced her to take sleeping pills. But even then, when she was too young to understand what it was, she still knew deep inside her that the spirit was a peaceful one; that the woman had died in her room years before and was lost, forever wandering the house and confused that a little girl was asleep in her bed. Years later, after they had moved house, Marlene had researched the lady who had been coming to her and she knew, by just having seen her and then discovering that she had died alone in bed, that she had helped the woman move on, that she had passed on to a better, more peaceful place.

But Lilly had shown her something else. Staring into the darkness of those eyes and seeing that almost fluorescent, beautiful face stare back at her, she knew that within her boiled a hatred and anger that could never be satisfied. Revenge alone was not enough for Lilly. Marlene shivered. She suddenly understood Jesse so much more now. How could he have grown up witnessing – feeling – so much pain and horror? Just to be in the presence of a vengeful spirit was something she could not describe in words. She now understood why he had spent his entire life running away and hiding from everyone, not forming relationships, not sharing anything about himself. A sadness rose up in her. Jesse had become like a son to her over these long months and she hated that he had spent so many years frightened of what was on the other side when she had only ever been blessed to see spirits as things of beauty and wonder. She was more determined than ever to save him from ever having to face evil again.

First she had to keep him away from Lilly, she couldn't let her take him as well.

CHAPTER FOURTEEN

James

By the time James had managed to find his phone and call the seafront office, his friends on the beach had completely lost sight of Jesse.

He came rushing back down the beach less than two minutes later and stood next to them, instantly soaked by a wave that crashed a few feet in front of him.

"We can't see him!" Little Bob screamed above the deafening wind to James as he came next to him.

"What the fuck do you mean you can't see him? He was there, we all saw him. He was fucking there by the silver ball!" James pointed out to where they had last seen Jesse.

"Well, he isn't now," Little Bob screamed back, the wind stealing his words before they reached the others.

James moved further forward towards the edge of the beach, closer to the tide as it came rushing in, the maelstrom threatening to drag him to his own death if he wasn't careful.

Geoff and Little Bob grabbed at him and held him back.

"He's there, he's got to be," James whispered as the adrenaline that had flooded his body a moment ago now started to drain away with the realisation of what must have happened.

"He's gone," Geoff said, the words barely leaving his lips.

They instinctively stepped back as the next wave screamed forward, their eyes no longer fixed on the silver ball, instead all looking at each other hopelessly.

Out of the darkened clouds came a beam of light as the coastguard helicopter flew over them and headed out to sea. All four heads at once looked up and followed it until it started hovering over the spot where Jesse was last seen.

"The coastguard!" Geoff screamed with hope suddenly restored.

"Brilliant, brilliant, fucking brilliant!" Mike shouted out to the others, a massive smile spreading across his face.

"I wasn't quick enough, was I?" James said as he turned away from them and headed slowly back up to the arch, barely noticing the wind and rain.

The other three kept their eyes fixed on the helicopter as it continued to hover over the pier, slowly moving over to the west and the beach next door.

"Look!" shouted Little Bob. "Over there, it's the lifeboat. They must have come from Shoreham."

At the same time as they spotted the lifeboat heading to the pier from the west, two coastguards were riding a yellow-striped buggy with flashing lights screeching to a halt outside the arch. The driver and passenger jumped out and ran towards the beach, almost colliding with James as they headed down to the others.

"Which one of you is James Hooper?" the driver asked the group.

"He's back at the arch," Little Bob answered him.

"Must've been the bloke we just went past," he said to his colleague. "You go back and take his statement; I'll talk to these three."

As his sidekick went back up the beach, his head low to avoid the wind and rain stinging his eyes, the driver turned to the others, his face ready to deliver the news that he had been trained to deliver.

Calling them over to him, he started his pre-prepared speech. "Guys, I'm Bryan Lynch, the seafront officer, you can call me

Lynch. Do you think we could go back to your club room? It'll be easier to talk there, less windy, I think." He had to scream to be heard above the noise of the waves. They nodded in unison, relieved to hand over authority to him.

Back at the buggy, they were reunited with James and Lynch's partner, Paul Jones. Like Lynch, Paul could have been plucked specifically for the job out of *Surfer's Monthly* magazine. Both stood at six foot one, with shoulder-length blond hair bordering on perm curly, sporting clean shaves, cut-off jeans and red jackets; if it had not been for the loss of his friend, James would have fallen about with laughter at the stereotypes.

"This is James Hooper, the one who phoned this in," Paul explained to his partner, talking as if the others were not there.

"I'll need all your names, please," Lynch said, taking out the iPad he had just retrieved from the glove compartment of his four-by-four.

"So, names first, please; including the person who's missing."

"I'm James Hooper." James took charge again. "This is Mike, Geoff and Little Bob; sorry, Bob," he corrected himself.

"And your friend; the one we're looking for?"

"Adam Austin," James said, looking down, unable to meet Lynch's eyes. "Adam, sorry, how do you spell his surname?" asked Lynch as he typed it into his iPad.

"What are you talking about?" Geoff blurted out before Mike or Little Bob could.

"What?" said James, looking up.

"It's Jesse Daniels, not Adam Austin. Jeeze," he said, rolling his eyes at James.

"Did I say Adam again?"

"Yes, you did. You've got to get a grip, man," Geoff carried on.

"Easy, Geoff," cut in Little Bob. "Sorry, Lynch, it's Jesse Daniels that's lost."

Lynch looked up at them. "Look, is it Adam or Jesse?" he

WHAT THE TIDE BRINGS BACK

asked them all. "This is serious. Someone's out there. This isn't a joke, you know. We've got men looking for him, putting their own lives at risk."

"It was a mistake, all right!" shouted James. "I meant Jesse, OK? It's Jesse Daniels."

"Adam died about five years ago," Little Bob tried to explain. "There was a storm then as well. They said it was suicide."

"Bob." James shook his head at his friend, not wanting to delve into Adam's death right now.

"So do you think Jesse…" – Lynch looked down at his notes – "Daniels was suicidal as well, then?"

"Adam wasn't suicidal," James shot back. "And neither was – is – Jesse."

Lynch shook his head and went back to his notes. Suddenly Paul's radio sprang to life, causing them all to jump.

"We've got him, Paul. Tell Lynch he's alive. He came out of nowhere. We'd almost given up and then he was there, he just popped up out of nowhere."

The voice from the radio filled the small room in the arch.

Lynch grabbed Paul's radio out of his hand before he had a chance to answer it himself.

"Coastguard, coastguard, Lynch here. Repeat, I say, repeat that."

"Lynch, it's Steve Lewis the coastguard from Shoreham. We've got him. He came out from under the pier, from nowhere. He was being tossed about quite a lot, he's taken in a fair bit of water and he's suffering from mild hyperthermia, but other than that, nothing's broken and he's fully conscious. The chopper winched him out and dropped him onto our deck. We're heading back to the station now. Hang tight, though, the chopper is going around again and the other lifeboat is nearly on scene. We think there might be another body out here."

Lynch looked at the men around him.

98

"Hold on, coastguard." He turned to the others. "Could there be someone else out there?" he asked, his tone suspicious and angry. "Well?" his voice rose.

"Who?" James asked, looking at the others.

"I'll check the ladies' room," Geoff said as he ran out the door into the smaller room opposite.

"Lynch, this is coastguard one. Do you have anything for us?"

"One second, coastguard," Lynch replied.

"Nothing," Geoff said coming back into the room. "The light was out and there're no bags, nothing. No one else from here went in."

"Negative, coastguard one, negative. No one else is missing."

"He keeps mumbling about someone called Lilly. Saying he followed Lilly in."

Lynch looked to the guys again, but each one shook their heads. As the name registered in James's head, he felt a sickness in his stomach; it was the same person that Adam was obsessed with, a name he had tried desperately hard to forget.

"Negative, coastguard one. Maybe Lilly was a pet dog he followed; it wouldn't be the first time."

"OK, Lynch. I'll tell coastguard two and the chopper, just in case. I doubt they'll stay out there long as it's not calming down and pretty soon it'll be too dangerous for them as well. I'm heading to Shoreham; we'll get this one straight to the hospital there, just in case."

"Thanks, Steve. I'll tell them here. I'll get one of them to come collect him. Over."

"Over," came the reply from the radio before it went silent once again.

Lynch handed the radio back to Paul.

"Your friend's got a guardian angel, guys. I thought he was a goner, if I'm honest, especially in that sea. Any of you know Shoreham Hospital?" he asked them.

The news that Jesse was still alive was slowly sinking in.

"I know the way," James replied, giving the others an 'I can't believe it' look. "I'll go get him."

"I'd leave it today, mate. He's probably suffering from hyperthermia having been in for so long in that temperature. Go first thing tomorrow. Does he have any family – a wife or kids – who should be notified?"

"There's no one," Geoff said.

James nodded his agreement, relieved he wouldn't have to face Jesse any time soon. Now that he knew Jesse was safe, the anger was starting to build in him that he had been crazy enough to go into a sea like that.

CHAPTER FIFTEEN

Marlene

Marlene had been calling Jesse for the last two hours, but his phone kept going straight to voicemail. She had left six messages so far, each one more urgent than the last. Finally, she decided to go to his house and simply pound on the door until he woke up and let her in. She had wanted to phone him the night before, once she had got back from London, but her mind was still too jumbled to make any real sense of it all and her head had started to throb once the paracetamol that she'd been given had worn off. She started calling him the moment she had woken up at five in the morning. She knew that time and etiquette played no part in Jesse's life and calling him so early in the morning would be no big deal.

In her car on the way to his flat, it dawned on her suddenly that it was already morning and Jesse would likely be at the beach having his swim. She grabbed two more painkillers from her bag on the passenger seat and took them dry as she pointed her car in the direction of Brighton Beach instead. The drive from her house in Hurstpierpoint to Brighton seafront at that time in the morning only took fifteen minutes down the A23 and she pulled into a space near Palace Pier just after seven-fifteen. She rushed down the slope from the seafront road to beach level and to the entrance of the swimming club arch. Since she had known him, she had never intruded on his time at the arch. She hesitated outside the door, wondering if coming here was a good idea. The shutter was raised, which meant someone was definitely here, but the glass door was shut, allowing her a clear view in but no means of access without knocking. She stared at the door, wondering how he would react to her being there. Despite all the times they had spent together at her home or at his flat, and all the secrets they shared, this was the one place he had never invited her to see. It was his place. Somewhere away from the ghosts in his head. But Lilly had changed that. It was no longer safe for him to be here; she needed to tell him that, she had to get him away from there.

The door to the arch opened and five people, all in their swim clothes, hovered in the hallway. Jesse was not with them.

"Erm…" she hesitated.

Suddenly being there, fully clothed in front of five partially dressed strangers, felt more awkward than she could have imagined.

"Can I help you?" a lady asked her.

"I'm looking for Jesse Daniels." Marlene found her voice.

A man stepped forward.

"Sorry, who are you?" he asked. "Are you from the council? Is it about yesterday?" he asked tentatively.

"I'm just a friend of Jesse's," Marlene replied, not picking up on the man's comment or nervousness. "I've been trying to get him on the mobile all morning and then I remembered he would probably be here. Is he?" she asked, looking around at them.

"No, sorry, we haven't seen him this morning. If you give me your name I'll write it in the diary in case he comes in later," the man said, not leaving his place at the door, blocking Marlene coming in or anyone else leaving.

Marlene was surprised by the way the man was acting towards her and she hesitated as this was not the answer she was hoping for.

"Um, I'm Marlene, can you just say Marlene is looking for him?"

"Sure, no worries."

The man turned back, pushing the door shut as he went, keeping a barrier between her and them.

Marlene wasn't one to be easily ignored. She stayed where she was until the door opened again and all five stepped out onto the seafront.

"Excuse me," she addressed the two ladies rather than any of the men. "Would you mind telling me when you last saw Jesse? It's really important I speak to him."

"You were here yesterday when it happened, weren't you, James?" one of the ladies chipped in.

"I'm not sure we should say anything, Sarah," James replied.

"Say what? What's happened to him?" Marlene's voice was suddenly filled with fear.

Sarah picked up on her distress and was quick to put her mind at rest. "He's fine, isn't he, James?" Sarah said.

"He's fine, just a bit shaken, that's all." James stepped forward.

"What happened?" Marlene asked, the worry etched into her voice clear for anyone to pick up on.

Sarah took Marlene's arm and led her around James into the arch ladies' section and sat next to her on the bench. James followed them in and stood opposite them.

"What happened?" Marlene asked.

Marlene saw Sarah look to James who looked around to see if any of the others had followed them in.

"I just need to know he's OK," Marlene persisted.

"It was yesterday morning," James started. "Me and the guys came to the beach for a swim. We didn't know he was here when we went in."

"It was pretty nuts out there, wasn't it? Not like this morning."

Marlene could feel the awkwardness in the room and realised that Sarah felt she had to say something rather than sit there compliantly. She looked between them, they were both in their costumes, a fishing knife was strapped to Sarah's right leg and a swimming cap covered her head. Marlene felt completely out of her comfort zone.

"I wasn't here myself, actually. Do you mind, James, if I leave it to you?" Sarah stood up. "Sorry about Jesse," she said to Marlene. "He'll be fine, I'm sure."

She smiled thinly and walked from the room, leaving James and Marlene alone.

"For God's sake." Marlene stood up and placed her hands on her hips, standing face to face with James like an angry school mistress. "Are you going to tell me what the hell's happened or not?"

"Sorry, of course," James said, trying to tear his eyes away from hers.

Marlene sat down and slid back on the bench until she hit the wall to give him some space and a chance to explain.

James told her everything that had happened.

"Is he hurt?" she asked, worried and relieved in equal measure.

"They didn't say. It's a bloody miracle he's even alive, though, we all thought he'd drowned." James shook his head. "They probably just want to keep an eye on him physically, but also I think they have to get someone, you know, to just have a word and see if he was suicidal, or anything."

"He's not suicidal," Marlene said with an edge to her voice.

"I never said he was, did I?" James replied. "I'm just saying they probably just need to rule it out, that's all. Anyway, he's there now, I was going to have a swim this morning and then head over there."

"Did you know Adam Austin?" Marlene threw it in without warning, catching James completely off guard.

"It wasn't the same as that, I never actually saw Adam in the water." He stood up from the bench, suddenly defensive.

Marlene also stood.

"Look, I'm worried about Jesse, that's all, and I'm pretty sure it's got something to do with what happened to Adam. So I'm just trying to understand, OK?"

"Who are you?" James asked accusingly.

"I'm just a friend of Jesse's. I'm his teacher, actually."

"His teacher? He never said he was studying anything. Teacher of what exactly?"

"I'm a spiritualist, or medium if you prefer. Jesse has a gift, a unique gift, and I'm helping him understand it. But Jesse has seen something, something dangerous, and I believe it's caught up with whatever happened to Adam Austin." She paused, trying to give James time to let this sink in.

After a moment, seeing the incredulous look on James's face, she continued, "Can you at least tell me what you know about Adam Austin? Even if you don't believe everything I'm saying, just believe that what I'm asking will really help Jesse. Please, James, I need your help."

"Actually, I don't believe in any of this psychic crap or whatever you call it. But if it'll help Jesse then sure, why not, it's not exactly private information. I'll tell you what I know, but then you can leave me alone, I really don't want to get caught up in whatever you and Jesse think is going on."

"Thank you. I've just a few questions…"

"Not here, not like this," he said, gesturing to his skimpy multicoloured Speedos. "Wait outside, I'll put on some clothes, we'll go to the coffee shop around the corner and I'll tell you everything. Just give me a minute."

"I know where Coffee Story is, Jesse told me you all go there," she said. "I just need half an hour with you, that's all, and then I'll go and get Jesse from the hospital and give him hell for putting us all through this."

Fifteen minutes later, they were tucked into the corner of the coffee shop away from everyone else. They waited in silence for their coffees to be delivered to their table.

"Cappuccino, no chocolate, extra hot, and a lemon tea?" the waitress asked.

"Mine's the coffee," James said. The waitress put the drinks down and walked away.

He took a small sip of his steaming cappuccino, settled back into his chair and sent her a look suggesting he really did not know where to start. Marlene had seen this reaction before lots of times when she was asking people about someone they had lost. Usually they were desperate to talk and yet at the same time felt vulnerable, even stupid, discussing in the open things that they only thought about in private, so they tried to tell her as little as possible. But they always gave it all up in the end. Spirits and ghosts were things she knew most people wanted to believe in; a life after death, perhaps a lasting existence of peace and love in the afterlife was something that, truth be told, many people wanted someone to convince them of. But they worried they would be laughed at if they said they believed. She knew the best thing to do was be patient and let them come to it in their own time, which they always did. Always.

James was no different. It took him nearly fifteen minutes and many micro sips of his coffee before he gave up, but when he did, the floodgates opened.

"Adam was my swimming buddy," he started. "We always buddy up in the club; safety in numbers, especially if you're out deep, or swimming around the pier or to the red buoy and back, that sort of thing, he was a strong swimmer. A bit like Jesse, actually, a natural sea swimmer. Probably one of the fastest in the club. I'm not exactly a slouch myself; I swam for the county when I was a kid and I've done a channel relay, but he could leave me standing if he wanted to. He never did, though; he always held back a bit to stay with me. We swam together at least four times a week, never Mondays, he always swam earlier on Mondays, but the rest of the week we'd go around the pier together when the temperatures picked up. Always shoulder to shoulder. Sometimes, though, he'd stray a couple of metres in front just to make me work hard, but he'd never leave me. He could have done, but he never did."

"So, what changed?"

"It was weird. One day, we got back from our swim and he was really coughing a lot; couldn't stop. He swore someone in the club was wearing some perfume or had been using a spray deodorant; we don't tend to do that in the arch as it's too small in there and people don't like it. I never smelt it, though; none of us did. It happened a lot after that, he'd come in coughing and would complain about it, but after a while it stopped making him cough; in fact, he even started to get really uppity if it wasn't there. He'd come in after a swim and say things like, "Where's she got to?" or he'd go to the beach and call out her name."

"Lilly?" Marlene asked, feigning surprise.

"Yes, that's right, Lilly. That's the thing," James said. "He didn't know a Lilly; well, not as far as I knew. And there wasn't a Lilly in the club. He started to talk about her a lot to me, it was weird. He'd talk about her as if she had once been there, you know, rather than in the present tense, and at other times he'd talk about her as if he had just been with her. It got odd. He started carrying around a diary as well, an old leather one and a pencil; he was really precious about it. No one was allowed to touch it. Or even look at it. Once he actually screamed at Sarah because he'd left it by the sink when he went in for a swim and she had picked it up to have a nose. She was only admiring it, but he went nuts, shouting at her, pushing her. She was in tears, and you could hardly blame her. He was almost asked to leave the club completely. If he hadn't apologised and put it right with her I think that would have been it for him. It was so out of character, though. If you'd known him you'd understand. After he died, the police tried to paint him as someone he wasn't, someone disturbed who had gone and committed suicide, but he wasn't, it wasn't like that. Up until the last six months, before he started talking about this Lilly, he was the nicest, funniest, kindest person I think I'd ever met. He had it all. A beautiful wife – Natalie, she was great. They had twins, they were only little when he died, it was heartbreaking, a boy and a girl. He had a really good business as well, over thirty staff selling mortgages and insurance. And they had an incredible house near the edge of the city, and lots of holidays, they were always away somewhere or planning the next one. He really had it all. Then suddenly everything changed, he seemed to lose it completely. I don't know what happened, just that everything about him seemed to change."

"Tell me about Lilly," Marlene gently asked, trying to keep him on subject but not spook him.

"Nothing I can say, I never met her," he said, looking up at Marlene for the first time. "She wasn't real, was she? He imagined her, didn't he?"

"I think she was real, James. Certainly to Adam she was real. And she certainly was real once."

"Is she a ghost?" he asked so quietly that she had to strain to hear him and, as he spoke, his head went down to his cappuccino rather than engage eye to eye with her or anyone else who was sitting nearby and might have heard his question.

"I think she's a spirit," Marlene said. "A spirit that needs closure but can't get it. I think that she had something to do with Adam's death. And I think she's come back again."

James looked up startled. "For Jesse?" he asked, suddenly scared.

"I don't think so, well not exactly. But I think Jesse is in her way and she needs to stop him interfering, and that scares me. Tell me more about Adam. What exactly happened to him?"

He looked down again into his cup.

"All I know is that I got to the arch one morning, it was just like yesterday, a crazy storm. But much worse than yesterday actually, much worse. There were six of us there at seven o'clock; the usual crowd. We knew we wouldn't get in from the start, so we agreed to have a groin shower."

"A groin shower?"

James smiled at Marlene. "We stand at the end of the groin in our costumes. Heads down, arms out straight holding onto the end of the groin as the waves crash over us. It's amazing! The waves go right over our heads and the sea just crashes down on us like a freezing cold shower. It's heavy as well – the water, that is. You're almost pushed to your knees."

Seeing Marlene's expression, he realised, as ever, that unless you're in it you don't get it.

"I know it sounds nuts," he continued. "But it's invigorating."

"And Adam was with you, for that groin shower that morning?" she encouraged him on.

"No, he wasn't, not that morning. We waited an extra five minutes for him but as we were just about to leave the arch, Geoff spotted his bag on the bench in the corner. It's funny thinking about it now, but Jesse sits in the same corner Adam did. Anyway, none of us had seen it when we first got there. We all ran out down the beach when we saw it. Just the same as yesterday," he said, shaking his head. "But we couldn't see him. Between us we covered both beaches either side of the pier, but it was crazy out there. Even the coastguard couldn't get out. When we checked at the arch, all his clothes were in the bag, everything you'd leave when you were swimming. That's how we were sure he'd gone in; his swimming stuff wasn't there."

"And the coastguard couldn't find him?"

"It was too dangerous for them to launch."

"Did they ever find his body, you know, afterwards?"

"No. Nothing, nothing at all. You don't always, actually. The tides can drag you way out to sea or miles and miles along the shore."

109

"Then how do you definitely know he went in? I mean, apart from his bag?" Marlene asked, wondering if perhaps they had got it so wrong and he had actually just upped and left.

"They found the note he left; and his diary."

"What note?" she asked, intrigued.

"The police said it was a suicide note; they kept it for a while and then gave it to Natalie. They suggested Adam might have been having an affair, but Natalie wouldn't have it. She refused to take the letter from them. But I saw it before anyone did. It was in his bag when I opened it after he first went missing. It was addressed to me, actually. It said Lilly wanted him. That she was coming for him; and then she was coming after the twins."

Marlene sat back, letting James catch his breath. She realised that he suddenly needed to tell it all now, he really needed to tell someone after five years of holding it all in.

"He said he had to stop her getting his babies and the only way was to go and find her. He went into that mental sea looking for this girl, like she'd be in the sea anyway! Can you believe it? Anyway, he went in and never came back, that's all I know. The police took the letter and the bag before anyone else could have a look. They questioned us all about this Lilly but none of us knew who she was. The police couldn't find anything about her and eventually they told the coroner that he'd left a suicide letter, that maybe he had been having an affair and that he was clearly unstable. But he wasn't unstable. And he wouldn't have had an affair, he loved Natalie too much." James looked up at Marlene again, seemingly ready to defend his friend if he needed to. "It was her, wasn't it? The same one Jesse mentioned to the coastguard yesterday when they pulled him from the sea. You think this Lilly... you think she's a ghost, don't you?" he almost laughed again saying it out loud. "You think she's a ghost who dragged him into the sea and drowned him?"

"Yes, I do," she replied seriously.

Marlene was the one person who actually could confirm it; or certainly felt she was qualified to.

"And I think she's back now, James. But I don't think it's Jesse she wants. I think maybe she's come back for Adam's twins after all, to finish what she started."

"Even if I did believe all this, what do you expect me to do?" James asked her.

"I need you to tell Jesse everything you just told me. And we have to find Adam's wife, Natalie, and warn her."

"I can't."

"Can't what? Which bit can't or won't you help me with?" Marlene asked challengingly.

"I can't talk to Natalie about this, I just can't. You never saw the way she looked at me after Adam was lost. She blamed me. Blamed all of the swimming club, actually; but mostly she blamed me. I should have been with him; I should have stopped him." James's head went down in his hands as he sat at the table in the coffee shop with a partial stranger and cried for the loss of his best friend.

The waitress cautiously walked over to their table but Marlene signalled her to leave them alone.

Ignoring the people around them whose sudden silence and curiosity had caused the noise to vanish from the coffee shop, Marlene took his hands in hers and squeezed them tight.

"You couldn't have stopped him, James. You couldn't have stopped him any more than he could have stopped Lilly. But we can stop her now. We can stop her taking Natalie's children in the way she took their dad. And we can stop her from destroying Jesse."

James brought himself back to sitting and dried his eyes with the back of his hand. The tears were gone now, replaced by something closer to determination.

"How can *we* stop her?" he asked seriously.

"I don't know if *we* can, but I know that Jesse can," Marlene said. "Jesse has seen her; felt her presence. And now she's seen him. And she's scared of him, of what he can do to her. James, I need you to tell Jesse everything. I'll find a way to help Jesse get to Adam's family and I'll give Jesse all the tools he needs to stop Lilly. But I need you to speak with Jesse and tell him everything you told me."

"I'll try to."

"I need you to do more than that. These are Adam's children we're talking about. You said you should have been there for Adam; well now's your chance."

From the expression she saw on his face it seemed as if the weight of the world had settled on his shoulders, and Marlene didn't know him well enough yet to know if he was strong enough to take it. She hoped he was.

"I'll speak with Jesse," he said.

"We'll go to him together, OK? You said he was at the hospital, right? So, that's where we'll start."

"Sure," James said. "But I have a lot of patients this morning and I need to reschedule them."

"Can't you do it from the car?" Marlene said strongly as she pushed back her chair and walked away from the table, heading for the door.

He had no choice but to follow in her wake.

Marlene drove and, apart from James calling his dental surgery to cancel all his appointments for the day, they drove in silence. It wasn't the awkward silence of strangers; it was a silence filled with tension.

Marlene pulled into the car park in front of Shoreham Hospital and drove straight into a space by the entrance.

A lady in her late sixties with a tired expression manned the reception desk. She was talking on the phone and motioned to them with her eyebrows to take a seat until she had finished her conversation. Holding their silence, they each took a seat. Over the following twenty minutes, the receptionist's eyebrows stayed busy as she continued the same call while managing to direct six other couples over to the line of chairs by her desk with just a look. James and Marlene sat in silence as the room started to fill with the voices of impatient families wanting to see their loved ones.

"Marlene? James?"

They both turned to see Jesse standing there, a look of confusion on his face.

"What are you two doing here? And how come you're together? I didn't know you knew each other?"

They stood up in unison.

"We need to talk, Jesse," Marlene said.

"We really do, mate," James cut in.

Jesse looked from one to the other, not quite sure what to make of it. "Let's get out of here then," he said as he walked towards the door.

"Are you free to leave?" James called after him as both he and Marlene followed past the reception desk. The receptionist, still on the phone and ignoring the rants coming from the ever-growing line of visitors, tried to slow them down and call Jesse back with a mixture of eyebrow ups and downs plus the addition of a nodding head, but that was a battle she would have lost even if she had applied her voice to the occasion.

Jesse spotted Marlene's car out in front and headed straight to the driver's side.

"I don't think so," Marlene said, stepping in front of him and opening the door as James headed straight for the front passenger seat and let himself in. "You can sit in the back, and just be grateful we came to get you."

"I'm grateful," Jesse replied with a sardonic grin.

As the car pulled away, James turned around to him. "I thought we'd lost you, mate. It was like Adam all over again. What the hell were you thinking going into a sea like that?"

"I'm sorry, James. You wouldn't understand, though, mate, it's complicated. Marlene, I don't know how you found James, exactly, and I'm not sure I even want to know, but I need to get home; then I think we need to talk."

"We almost had to go into the sea to fucking save you, Jesse." James turned to face him again, his expression furious.

"James, don't, please." Marlene tried to stop him, scared of how Jesse would react to being challenged so fiercely. She knew him well enough to know he had the propensity to blow at any moment.

She needn't have worried, though. "I'm sorry, mate," Jesse said sincerely.

"Sorry! Fucking sorry! Do you know we had to call the coastguard, and the helicopter? We thought you'd drowned, for Christ's sake. God knows how they found you in that mess, let alone got you on board. You should be dead by now. And how the hell did you just walk out of the hospital wearing that gown? Where're your clothes, man?"

Jesse couldn't help but smile at his friend.

"Jesse, I'm serious, man. You scared the life out of me."

"I get it," Jesse replied, calming James down with one of his smiles and a gentle shoulder pat from the back seat.

Marlene said nothing, she just drove on, happy that Jesse was not screaming at her to pull over.

"Let's just get me home so I can get some clothes on and I'll make us all a drink, and then we can chat."

They arrived at Jesse's flat twenty minutes later after a quiet, uneventful drive down the seafront road from Shoreham to Hove. With the parking gods still on her side, Marlene pulled into a space right outside Jesse's front door. "That's handy," Jesse said as they climbed out of the car, unaware that the gown had come undone and he was showing his rear end to anyone who happened to be passing by.

They went to the front door. Jesse stopped suddenly and exclaimed, "My keys! They're in my bag at the arch. Shit, I hope someone else is in."

He pressed the ground floor buzzer first and was relieved to hear Susie's voice.

"Susie, it's Jesse. I've forgotten my keys." The intercom buzzed the door open.

As they trooped into the hallway, Susie opened her door and she saw Jesse still dressed in the backless operating robe.

"What happened?" she asked.

"Not now, Susie. I'll call later," he said, walking right past her as if she was just another of his tenants.

Marlene and James said nothing, aware of the tension coming from Susie's glare, and carried on following him without catching her eye.

Six flights of stairs later, they came to Jesse's door. He tapped the four-digit code into the entry panel, and the door clicked open. As he let them in, he noticed the bruises and cuts on Marlene's face for the first time. He stopped her before she walked up the short flight of stairs from his front door to the main living space.

"What happened?" he spoke softly.

"You get changed and I'll make us all a coffee," she replied.

Jesse

Once they were all seated around the table in Jesse's lounge, Marlene told them everything that had happened at the British Library, from the information she'd found out about Lilly Baker and the Austin Hotel, to John Austin and her theory about him being the swimmer Jesse saw, and about the brutal murder at the orphanage and the likelihood that Lilly escaped a workhouse in London as a child and headed to the coast in Brighton.

She ended with the dramatic events on the escalator, when the last thing she remembered before she fell was the malevolent look on Lilly's face.

"She actually showed herself to you?" Jesse was visibly shocked and concerned.

"Yes, she did."

"You told me you never saw spirits, not since you were a child," Jesse said. "You've always described your gift as hearing and feeling, but never as seeing."

"Clairvoyance comes in different ways, Jesse; clairvoyance, clairsentience, clairaudient. My gift is more clairvoyance, but I'm not limited to that, we can cross over at times. You perhaps can control it and are equal with all of the gifts, but the rest of us can't do that, but it can still happen to us on occasion."

"But what you're suggesting is that she didn't just appear as a spirit like your lady in the bedroom wandering around unseeing, but that Lilly was actually there for you, to harm you in some way."

"Yes, I believe she was. It's the first time I've ever had that happen to me. It frightened me. But I don't think it was my gift that brought her to me. I think she did it herself. She's powerful, Jesse, I think she can appear to whoever she wants to and whenever she wants to."

"Excuse me, can you back up one minute?" James was completely lost. "What are you guys talking about; a clairwhatsit?"

"Clairvoyance, the ability to see spirits, clairsentience to feel spirits, clairaudient to hear spirits," Marlene explained, taking on the role of teacher once again while Jesse went into the kitchen to make more coffees.

"And which are you and Jesse, then?" James asked.

"Well, as I said, we both cross over all of them in truth, most mediums do, but we usually have one gift stronger than the other. For me, it's much more clairaudient – hearing spirits – but I was born clairvoyant. In fact, my first experience as a child was seeing the spirit of a lady who used to sleep in my bedroom. It was frightening as a child, I can tell you; then after a while, I simply stopped seeing her. Ever since then, I've only been in contact with spirits by voice and feel."

"Feel?" James said, confused once again. "What do you mean feel?"

"I *feel* my body change. It's like this; if a spirit comes to me I usually *feel* something before I hear anything. I could be sitting reading a book and all of a sudden my left foot could start to feel bigger. Not swollen as such, just bigger. Like it's not mine, that it's different to my right foot; bigger, bulkier, heavier even. Definitely not mine. Then I can sense a spirit near me, I get that feeling most people get but don't recognise – the one when you feel someone is behind you. And then I get a voice in my head. This voice will be different to mine, just like yours is different to mine. They'll be a different choice of words, maybe even the speed of the words as they come out, even an accent, but that's less easy for me to pinpoint. Sometimes I can't even understand what the words mean, yet the point of the sentence still comes through to me."

Jesse came back to the lounge with three fresh coffees, putting one in front of them all.

"You can do all this as well then, can you, Jesse?" James said, more of a statement than a question. "And which *Claire* do you favour?"

Jesse shot James an angry look.

"Marlene and I have work to do; if you're going to take the piss then just leave and let us get on with it."

"Jesse," Marlene barked at him.

"It's all right, I'm used to him by now," James responded, before turning back to Jesse. "If you think I'm taking the piss then you're wrong. You've had your whole life to get used to this, I've been at it for what" – he jokingly looked at his watch – "a few hours. Before Adam drowned I never believed anything like this, but since then, well, let's just say I have become more open-minded."

"What made you feel like that, James? Is there something else you've not told me?" Marlene asked him. "You told me yourself that Adam's death was recorded as suicide, but you never believed it. And when you and I talked about Lilly, I could see in your eyes that you never believed she was a real person in Adam's life. So what pushed you into thinking it was more than it seemed to be?"

"I think it was the diary. After I found it in his bag, I took it before the police saw it. I don't know why, exactly, it just felt like he was leaving it for me. I read some of it, I wish I hadn't. It felt really personal. He'd written it at the start for his children, as a kind of history for them about his sea swimming to look back on as they got older rather than as a diary for himself. It was really odd hearing him talk like that; he wrote as if he were speaking to it – it was unsettling."

"I always thought the police had taken the diary," Jesse said, the accusatory tone having left his voice as quickly as it had come.

"They only took the letter."

"The suicide letter?"

"It wasn't a suicide letter; it was a letter addressed to me. They read it like that because they hadn't read the diary first and never understood the full story. I read a lot of it. It changed halfway through. It stopped being a story from him to his kids and became more of a conversation between him and someone I thought was a real person, but it became clear she was in his imagination. I thought she was like a fake friend, you know, like kids have."

"Lilly?" Marlene asked.

"Yes, he called her Lilly. He wrote a lot about her. It was like he knew all about her but didn't actually know her as such. And as the days went on, he became really aggressive, in the diary and in real life. Angry, even. He seemed to think she was going to get him somehow. And then at the end, near the end anyhow, he decided she was going to get his children as well. That was when his writing got really crazy. He seemed to be shouting at her through the diary, challenging her somehow to come and get him and leave them alone. He put a loose page in the diary just for me, telling me that he was going to find her in the sea. He wasn't going in to die, it was to find Lilly and stop her. At least that was what he was suggesting."

"And you didn't think to show it to the police? Or his wife?" Jesse was incredulous.

"And tell them what, Jesse? That Adam had a friend in his head who was trying to kill him and his family. For Christ's sake, he was already dead when I found it. Letting them think he had gone into the sea to find a ghost, how the hell would that have helped?"

"Well it couldn't have been as bad as them thinking it was suicide, could it?"

"Leave it, Jesse. James is right; it wouldn't have helped at the time. He did what he thought was right, that's all any of us can ever do. Where's the diary now, James?"

"I gave it to Natalie after the funeral. I'd taken out the page he'd written to me and torn it up, but I couldn't destroy the diary, it wasn't mine to do that. So I gave it to her. I told her to read it."

"She obviously didn't read it, did she?" Jesse said. "Or if she did she didn't take it seriously. If she had, she might have sold up and left, got away from here and taken the children somewhere safe."

"She couldn't run from this, Jesse, you should know that better than anyone, you can't escape your fears by running away, you have to face them or they just go with you," Marlene cut in.

"It's not the same!" Jesse shot back at her. "Has she got the diary still?" he asked James.

"I've no idea. She snatched it from me and then slammed the door in my face. She blames me, all of us at the club, actually. Perhaps, she's right. Maybe I could have done more to help him."

"You couldn't have done anything," Marlene said to comfort him as he shook his head again and the tears started to form in his eyes once more.

James stared intensely at Jesse.

"What?" Jesse shot at him, suddenly irritated at the way his friend was staring at him.

"Why do you think you can stop her if Adam couldn't?" James said to Jesse.

Marlene answered for him. "Jesse is different," she stated.

"Different, how?"

"Give me your phone," she said to James.

He looked at her for a second longer than usual before he typed in the code and then handed it over.

Marlene opened the photos app and selected one at random.

120

She showed James the one she had chosen and then put the phone face down on the table.

"What is it, Jesse?" she asked.

Without hesitation, Jesse said, "Flowers."

"What type?"

"Soft flowers, nothing big."

"Colour?" Marlene asked.

Jesse looked down at the back of the phone.

"Don't look," Marlene scolded him. "Instinct only."

"Blue," Jesse replied.

Marlene turned over the phone. The picture facing them was a row of flowers, hyacinths, iris, lobelia and shrubs taken from James's garden. The colours were mixed, but there was blue running through them all.

James said nothing. He picked up the phone and looked at the picture again, before looking back at Jesse and then Marlene.

"Choose another one," she said.

James lowered his eyes from Jesse to his phone and scrolled through over a thousand photos he had stored. He stopped at one that would mean nothing to James or Marlene, turned off the screen and put the phone back in his pocket.

Jesse kept his eyes firmly on James and without hesitation said, "A house."

"What type of house?" Marlene asked.

Again with no hesitation Jesse replied, "It's not straight exactly. I can see lines. It's a house, though, but not straight."

James said nothing; he just kept looking at Jesse trying to work out how he did it. James took the phone back from his pocket and put it face up on the table and typed in the security code. It was a picture of James and his two children at a farm, and in the background stood an old farmhouse built of stone, the walls sagging with age and creating a criss-cross of lines where the stones had moved over the ages.

"Jesse, tell me about James's bedroom," Marlene asked.

"He's never even been to my house," James said suspiciously.

"It's upstairs," Jesse said instantly. "Front of the house, I think. There are two single beds, they make a double, but it's not a double. Curtains that aren't curtains, I'm not sure what I mean by that… not blinds, though, I don't know for sure, but not curtains. And a desk? Not a work desk, though, kind of like a roll desk. Something old. And swirls on the carpet."

"What colour are the curtains?" Marlene asked.

"Brown," Jesse said. "But not curtains," he emphasised again.

"Well?" Marlene said to James.

James looked from one to the other before replying.

"There were two single beds in there when Jayne and I moved in and we pushed them together, but we changed them for a double last year. And we used to keep my grandmother's old bureau in there, but it's in the spare room now."

"And curtains and carpets?" Marlene asked.

"The carpet is old; we haven't changed it yet. It's really patterned, definitely swirls and circles. And we don't have curtains or blinds; we have brown tie backs. Curtains but not curtains, I guess."

"Anything else, Jesse?" Marlene turned to him.

"That watch you lost, the one from Edna, it's fallen behind a unit, a vanity unit or something."

"Who's Edna?" Marlene asked.

"She's his family. No, that's not right, she's not family. Well she's family but she's not. I feel a little sick as well." Jesse put his hand to his throat. "And I've butterflies in my stomach, like when you're really nervous. Who's Edna?" he asked James.

James had gone white.

"It wasn't Edna," James said. "It was Ethel. And she was my wife's mother, my mother-in-law. She died a couple of years ago of stomach cancer. She was sick most days, she couldn't keep anything down. We lost her watch months ago; Jayne has been looking everywhere for it; it meant a lot to her. How did you do that, Jesse? How could you know all that just by sitting there?"

"He just knows," said Marlene. "The accuracy he has is off the charts; I've never seen anything like it. They were simple things, though. I've put him through tests that I've only ever read about in old books that shouldn't be possible and he flew through them. I've only ever read one book that documents someone with gifts like Jesse, it's not even a book actually, just papers. They're really old, and I'm talking Biblical old. There was this lady, she was called a ghost hunter. I can't read it myself as it makes no sense to me, the drawings are meaningless, but to Jesse they form words, stories. She was said to have been able to do fantastical things."

"What happened to her?" James asked, while Jesse sat impassively, his frustration starting to build.

"The last story Jesse could find that was written about her, about eight hundred years ago, depicts her being taken into the spirit world by a vengeful spirit who was as powerful as she was. There's a picture of her, it hangs in the Louvre in Paris – most people don't realise the subject matter. But it's there all the same."

"So you believe in all this, then?" James said, forgetting in part who he was talking to.

"I'd heard rumours over the years and read fables about a mystical ghost hunter, but no, I never believed them." Marlene turned to look at Jesse. "But I never knew Jesse back then."

"For Christ's sake. I am not some mystical fucking ghost hunter suddenly reborn in modern day Brighton. So, can we forget the bloody theatrics and get back to what we are here to talk about: Lilly, Adam and his daughter."

"I needed James to understand what you can do, Jesse," Marlene said. "It's important if we're going to work together on this."

"Who said we needed to work together? Look, James, stay or

don't stay, I couldn't care less at the moment. In fact, I think it's best if you don't stay."

"I'm just trying to help, mate," James said.

"Well, you're not helping, are you? If anything, you're in the way now. Just leave it to us, all right." Jesse pulled himself up to standing to signal that it was time James left.

"Fine, if that's the way you want it," James replied. "Good luck with him, Marlene," he said as he headed for the door. "You're welcome to him and all this crap." He turned back to Jesse as he walked through the door. "And stay out of the sea, I might not be there next time to save your arse."

With that, he stormed out, slamming the door behind him.

Marlene looked at Jesse over her glasses and slowly shook her head at him in frustration as he sat back down.

"Well, that was smart, Jesse. So now we've got limited information on Adam, no friends at your swimming club and Lilly to deal with on our own. Or maybe you want to do this without me as well."

"Don't you get it, Marlene?" Jesse turned to her. "She showed herself to you! You can't deal with her like I can. She's dangerous. I can't protect you both from her."

"You don't know that."

"I do know that! I wasn't there, was I, at the library. She could have killed you, for Christ's sake. I can't take that risk."

"It's not your choice, Jesse. We're in this together. You have no idea how powerful you are and absolutely no way of knowing how to control what you can do. You need me now more than ever."

"I don't need you, or anyone. I can deal with Lilly on my own and I can save Adam's daughter on my own."

"Why do you keep saying Adam's daughter? He's got twins, a boy and a girl."

"Because it's the girl that Lilly is after."

"How can you know that?"

"Because I saw her when I went to Adam's house. She was in the window looking at me. And I'd seen her before."

"In your dreams?" Suddenly Marlene understood what Jesse was getting at. "Adam's daughter is the girl in your dreams, isn't she?"

"Yes."

"What happened to you yesterday, Jesse?"

"I went to Adam's house to see his wife, but she didn't open the door. I saw the girl, though. Then it kind of all went blank. I don't remember much after that."

"You don't remember going to the beach? Or going into the storm?"

"I remember some bits. I was outside the girl's house and I remember starting to cough, it felt like I was breathing in a perfume and it was burning my throat. I vaguely remember getting on my bike and heading down their road. But after that it's sketchy. I can't really remember much."

"Do you remember the smell of the perfume? Was it sweet and bitter at the same time? Really far in the back of your throat, tickling it and scratching it."

"That's right. How could you know that?" he asked, leaning forward on the table.

"I had the same thing on the escalator. It made me dizzy it was so strong. It was Lilly, wasn't it, it's her perfume we both smelt?"

"Let's just leave it there," Jesse said. "I don't want to talk about this any more."

"You've got to, Jesse. I need to know everything you know."

"I don't know what I know, that's the point. I can't remember anything. One minute I was outside the house and the next I was being pulled from the sea. I remember feeling scared, standing outside the house, just before it all went blank. If I had to swear on it, I'd say I was feeling someone else's fear, though. Adam's maybe, I don't know—" Jesse stopped abruptly as a memory emerged.

Marlene had been watching his face carefully. "What is it, Jesse?"

Jesse closed his eyes and tried to block out everything. There was something in his memory nagging at him.

"What is it, Jesse?" Marlene repeated. "What can you see? Is it Lilly, or Adam, or the girl?

Jesse continued to sit there, his eyes tightly closed, his breathing slow. "Come on, Jesse, think hard, concentrate. Tell me where you are, what can you see?"

"It was Lilly. She was waiting for me at the house. She took me to the arch. I couldn't stop her; I don't think I wanted to stop her. She was taking me back to her time and I couldn't stop her doing it, she had complete control over me." Jesse opened his eyes and looked at Marlene. "Did I want to go with her? Why did I let her lead me into the sea like that? Is that what she did to Adam? Am I just like him? I thought I was stronger than that," Jesse said, disappointed in himself.

Marlene was frightened.

"We still don't know what you can or can't do with your powers, Jesse, we don't even know what control you have. For all we know, Lilly could have taken you back to the 1800s and kept you there; and then what? Or you could have drowned. It's all too much. We can't fight her like this, it's impossible. We need to understand what she wants before you can face her again. You need to keep away from her, from the arch, and the sea. You can't go back again, you mustn't."

She had raised her voice like a mother trying to get through to a stubborn child.

"What about Adam's kids? I can't just let Lilly come back and take them."

"She's too strong for us right now, Jesse. We don't know how to fight her. No, absolutely not, I won't allow it, you need to stay away. Until we know what you can do, we both need to stay away."

"I'm sorry, but you need to stay away, not me."

"We're in this together, Jesse, you need me if you're going to stop Lilly, you can't do this on your own."

"I need no one; I've told you that time and again. In fact, I think it's time you went as well."

He stood up, signalling the meeting was over. "Jesse, don't," she pleaded.

"Just go away, Marlene. I don't need you any more, you've taught me all you can now, you've nothing left I need. I can do this on my own."

"Jesse, you've so much more to learn; you're not ready for her. I can still help you."

"Help me! I asked you to help me before and you didn't. I asked you to show me how to reach my family. I begged you to show me how to reach my dad, but you wouldn't, would you? Or you couldn't. Either way, the one time I needed you, you let me down. So why do you think I need you now?"

"I told you, it's not possible. You can't reach your dad; he'll only come through me. You're too close to him, it's not possible to do that."

"It's your way of controlling me, holding me back, and I've had enough of it. Just get out. I don't need you; I don't need James; I don't need anyone."

In frustration, Marlene stood up and grabbed her bag and moved towards the door.

"You need to grow up, Jesse. You can't treat people like this. Like it or not, you need friends around you. And I've just about had enough of this myself now. Look at me, I'm bruised and beaten up by a spirit who should not even be able to show herself to me and all you can do is sit there acting like a spoilt child. Well, maybe it's me who doesn't need this any more."

She slammed the door behind her as she left.

★★★

Jesse had never wanted to push Marlene away, or James for that matter. But after seeing what Lilly had done to Marlene, and what she had done to him, he had no choice but to do what he could to protect them both. He needed to get back to Adam's house and find that diary.

As he left the living room, Jesse looked up to the skylight straight into the clouds hovering under the deep blue sky, as if he could talk directly to Lilly.

"You want a fight, then let's have a fucking fight. But this time just you and me, Lilly. This time you can leave my friends alone."

CHAPTER SEVENTEEN

Marlene

Marlene was exhausted. She had tried to keep everything together, to keep Jesse focused, but now she simply felt overwhelmed by it all. Jesse had never spoken to her like that before and had never sent her away. She couldn't work out if he was doing it for her own good or if he really meant to push her away. She left Jesse's flat at breakneck speed, her car heading into the turns at a crazy fifty miles an hour. Like a floodgate bursting, everything hit her at once, and a tidal wave of emotion suddenly drowned her.

The first meeting with Jesse had only been a year ago; the voice from the spirit of his dad constantly in her head pushing her on, compelling her to help and protect his son; the unbelievable and rapid progress they'd made on his psychic ability, despite his reluctance to be part of the world she lived in; and now Adam's daughter, and Lilly Baker, and most of all the terrifying realisation that evil spirits really do exist. Marlene had always believed that spirits were made of pure energy, energy made of light and peace, who at worst were lost souls looking for help to move on, or simply a spirit searching for *the* answer. In her opinion, evil spirits were just fables told by old women to keep their grandchildren in line. Never in her wildest fears did she imagine that a spirit could, or would, seek vengeance. Or could kill.

That was until Lilly had shown herself, in the flesh, and it was only through luck that she hadn't died that night on the underground. The look in Lilly's eyes and the darkness that emanated from her had been clear; Marlene was meddling in Lilly's plans and that would not be tolerated. Others had died already at Lilly's hands; how many, she didn't yet know. There was the murder at the orphanage that she suspected was Lilly's doing and then the murder, or suicide, of Adam Austin over a hundred years after her death. But were there others in between? And if so, who and how many? And now Lilly was back and, if Jesse was right, it was for Adam's daughter. And right in the middle of it all was Jesse. So capable and so strong, but perhaps not strong enough – not yet, anyway. Certainly not strong enough to stop Lilly. Only she had the patience and skills to help him. She knew it instinctively, from the first time Jesse's dad had spoken to her to the moment she had first stood next to Jesse himself, she'd known. He was special, one of so few amongst the billions of souls ever born who had the power to cross over between worlds. An ability to gaze into the past and shape the future. He just didn't know how to control it and he could not bring himself to believe how special he was. But she could help him, she could show him how to control his gift, and she could protect him from Lilly. She just didn't know if she had the strength to protect him from himself. He was so reckless, so angry and so unpredictable.

She slammed on her brakes as she drove into the next corner, the car screeching as it tried to stop. The tears were streaming down her face so fast that the windscreen had become a blur. She missed the sharp bend that came up suddenly on the B2117 Brighton Road to Hurstpierpoint and careened through the fence of Lattice Cottage; an abandoned farmhouse hidden from view behind an old fence that had witnessed many near misses on the same spot over the years. She killed the engine and fell forward, her head in her hands as her body shuddered under the stress of everything.

Thankfully, no one had been behind her or coming the other way as she had left the road, or she would have done the job for Lilly herself. The tears slowly stopped and her trembling shoulders eased as the realisation of the accident took hold.

Her car had come to a stop right outside the front door of the abandoned cottage. It was nestled privately within two acres, hidden from the B road that ran straight past it by an exhaust-damaged fence and old lumbering trees. The house itself looked solid and well kept, but the land around it was overgrown and boggy. The grass around the house was almost as high as the downstairs windows and the trees that landscaped the grounds were so large that their branches either reached high into the heavens or were bent down onto the soil, the weight of the years making them look like they were bowing low in front of royalty. The house itself stood to the east of the land, creating a large overgrown lawn to its west and an expanse that stopped at a small stream in front of it. The stream, which was fed from a neighbouring farm, ran into a small lake that was now more bog than water, and behind it to the south, running the full length of the land, was a forest of trees and bushes that backed directly on to the South Downs National Park; all overlooked to the south by the large mound that was Wolstonbury Hill. Behind which was Marlene's own home, out of her view now but protected by the same hill that she gazed at from her car.

Without thinking, she opened her door and got out. It felt as if she was being led from the broken fence, past the house and forward to the stream. Stepping through the long grass, her feet sinking into the boggy soil, she found herself at a small bridge that led from one side of the old lake to the woods on the other side. She had to cross it. It was not her choice, she was being led again; a feeling of a hand in her hand drawing her forward with urgency. Walking across the bridge, she was suddenly overcome with emotion. It wasn't the fear and stress that had caused her to crash through the fence just a couple of minutes ago; this was someone else's emotion. She recognised it easily, though. She had got used to this feeling over the last year. This was the feeling she got when Jesse's dad would show her a glimpse into Jesse's future, or his past. This time she felt peace and calmness surround her senses. These were not emotions his dad had ever shared with her before. Whenever he stood near her, he would only share with her the fears and worries that Jesse brought him from across the heavens, but never this; never peace and tranquillity. She felt Jesse here. Not right now, not with her physically. But some time in the future. She felt him in this spot, standing alone on this bridge, taking in the majestic view of Wolstonbury Hill as it stood guard over the national park with the warmth and safety of Lattice Cottage close behind him. The vision was fleeting, but so powerful. It felt like she was watching him from behind a tree. Witnessing a time in his life when he had found the peace and safety that were stolen from him in the car crash. Jesse's dad had brought her here, she felt that now. She closed her eyes and concentrated on the words trying to form in her mind.

This was going to be the Daniels' family home. Jesse's dad was going to buy the house as a surprise for the family, to move them from the middle of the city to a family home in the country just a few miles away. He had never told anyone about it, not even his wife or children. It was to be his surprise to them. But he died before it had ever happened. Jesse was robbed of that future on the day the car left the road. Tears crept down Marlene's face as she realised how much had been stolen from Jesse on the night his family died. He didn't just lose his family, but he lost a future that he would never now have. But that didn't mean he couldn't have a future, a happy and peaceful one.

Drying her eyes, she walked back across the bridge onto the boggy garden knowing what she had to do. She knew she couldn't

abandon Jesse now. He needed her even if he didn't realise it...
she couldn't give up on him now.

Pushing the fallen fence panels off her bonnet, she climbed
back into the car and started the engine, which by some miracle
fired up straight away. She pointed the car back towards Brighton
and pressed slowly on the accelerator as the tyres started to bite
into the boggy soil beneath. She needed to find James. She knew
he could help her, that he had something that would lead her to
Lilly Baker. If she was going to help Jesse, then the first step was
finding as much out about Lilly Baker as she possibly could –
perhaps the secret to stopping her in the future was finding out
about her past.

CHAPTER EIGHTEEN

Natalie

This morning, just as every other Sunday morning, Natalie woke to an empty bed, an empty room and an empty heart. Next to her should have been her husband, and five years on, that loss remained as painful as ever.

But next to her should also have been her children, Daisy and Alfie, snuggled up with her on a Sunday morning planning what fun things they should do for the day. But they didn't do that anymore. She looked at the clock next to the bed; it was nearly nine o'clock. She never slept in that late. Even without them in the bed with her, she always heard the television from the lounge downstairs – they always made themselves toast and watched television until she came down to say good morning. But there was no TV sound this morning; in fact, there was no sound at all.

Her heart momentarily slowed. Her breathing went silent. The house was quiet; completely and utterly quiet.

"Kids," she whispered. Then, "Daisy! Alfie!" she screamed, as the panic of being totally alone forced its way into her head.

Natalie scrambled out of bed and ran from her bedroom down the hall to the room next door. It was in darkness still, the lights off and the blinds shut. She flicked the light switch on, instinctively knowing that there would be no young eyes momentarily blinded by the glare. Despite knowing the room was empty, she still shouted out their names.

"Guys, please don't hide from me. Guys, please," she continued as she ducked down to the bottom bunk, ruffled the duvet, then pulled herself up to the top bunk and did the same.

"Guys, please," she repeated as she left Alfie's room and went further down the hallway to Daisy's room, which was already light from the morning sun. The blinds in Daisy's room were never closed and the bed, as right now, was always perfectly made and lined with teddies and dolls. Giving Daisy's room a cursory glance, she went back into the hall and along to the fourth and final bedroom; the room that might have become a nursery one day if Adam had not died. They had always planned on having three children and had built the house with three equal-sized children's rooms. The room, having never fulfilled its destiny, was now just a dumping ground for school uniforms, school bags and old toys that needed to be taken to the charity shops. It also held no children this morning.

"Kids, for Christ's sake, this isn't funny!" Natalie shouted from the hallway down the stairs.

The screech from the gate buzzer broke through the stillness in the house. "What the hell are they doing outside?" Natalie said to no one as she ran down the stairs, ignoring the fingerprints on the glass balustrades that would normally cause her to stop halfway down and start cleaning.

She hit the gate opener without considering that they would never have actually opened the gate and gone beyond the grounds without her. She pulled open the front door expecting to see them coming through the gate and bounding up the stairs into the house, full of mischief. But it was not the kids she saw standing at the foot of the stairs.

"Natalie Austin?" the man at the bottom of the stairs asked.

She momentarily forgot she was expecting to see the children and looked at the stranger. There was something familiar about him that she couldn't quite place. He had a similar build to Adam, standing at about five foot ten, slim but not skinny, broad shoulders and a T-shirt that looked as though it was hiding perfectly formed abs. He was better-looking than Adam had been, she thought guiltily. Adam had been a decent-looking man, some would say handsome even. But the stranger was stunning. His olive skin shaped a perfect face with just enough stubble to pull off a cool but not scruffy look. His eyes were a piercing blue and even at the distance from the front door to the bottom of the steps, the contrast between olive skin, dark brown hair speckled with grey and vivid blue eyes was breath-taking. As he slowly walked up the stairs to greet her, Natalie noticed the teardrop birthmark under his left eye; it lent a sadness to what otherwise would have been a happy face.

"Natalie Austin?" the stranger repeated.

Suddenly remembering why she was there, Natalie rushed down the stairs past the man, into the drive, frantically looking left and right before heading through the gate and searching up and down the street. Seeing no children, she turned back and ran up the driveway, staying to the right, and ran through the wooden side gate to the alley at the side of the house and sprinted up to the garden, stopping only when she reached the patio at the back of the house.

★★★

Jesse, now standing two thirds of the way up the stairs, didn't know what to make of it. Something was clearly wrong, though, and he didn't need his psychic powers to understand that. When he had first pressed the gate buzzer he had expected a voice to ask who was there, he hadn't expected the gate to just open. And when he tentatively walked through onto the drive and saw the front door open, he had not expected to see a half-dressed woman, her hair fanned out as if she had just fallen out of bed, looking straight through him and then running around as if he was not even there. Not quite sure what to do, he took the stairs back down, three at a time, and followed her through the side gate to the garden at the top.

The garden ran upwards from the patio at a gentle slope for about eighty feet, bordered on both sides by flowers and shrubs. A built-in outside BBQ kitchen was set onto its own patio halfway up, and at the top of the garden stood a magnificent three-piece freestanding treehouse. To the right, sunk into rubber matting, was a trampoline. It was a perfect mix of adult and child space. Natalie was standing next to the treehouse, her head turning this way and that. Jesse stood watching her for a moment. Even standing in flannel shorts and a top, her hair unbrushed and a look of pain and worry etched on her face, Jesse thought she looked incredible. Her nightclothes could not hide the perfect figure, her breasts pushing forward through the material and her legs, not a mark on them, running down from lightly muscled thighs to bare feet. Her red hair, despite having been slept on, curled up at the edges and had a slight wave to it. And even at this distance, her brown eyes were captivating. Jesse was rarely thunderstruck by someone's beauty; in truth, he didn't find physical beauty the most appealing thing about a woman, he was usually attracted to their personality before their appearance – the feistier the better, just like himself. But standing at the bottom of the garden looking up at Natalie, he was mesmerised.

"Daisy, come out now!" Natalie screamed to the garden, her voice no longer strong, but filled with the fear of a parent searching for a lost child. "Alfie, please, please…" she started to sob as she fell to her knees, her face in her hands.

Jesse heard the noise first and stepped a few paces forward off the patio onto the grass and then turned around and looked up, past the first and second floors.

"What's up there, Natalie?" he called behind him.

"Who are you?" she asked Jesse accusingly.

"What's in that room?" he continued. "The one at the very top."

"The gym," she said.

She followed his gaze and saw a window open at the top of the house.

She ran back down the garden, past Jesse, and pulled open the sliding patio doors that led into the lounge. She reached the top floor out of breath and pulled open the door to the gym. Alfie was lying on his back lifting a small weight above his head while Daisy hung upside down, suspended by her ankles on the circus rings from the pull up bar.

"Hi, Mum," they said in unison.

"Why didn't you say something when I called you?" she shouted at them.

"We didn't hear you," Alfie said, sitting up.

"Sorry, Mum. What's wrong?" Daisy asked, still hanging upside down.

"I… well, it doesn't matter. Didn't I say you shouldn't come in here on your own? It's dangerous with all these weights lying around."

"Dad never minded."

Natalie turned to Alfie and shouted, "Actually, he did mind. You were babies, for God's sake, you don't even remember him, do you?"

"I do remember him!" Alfie screamed back.

"Me, too," Daisy added, dropping herself onto the exercise mat and going over to sit with Alfie.

"You might not remember him, but we do," Alfie sneered at his mum.

"How dare you!" Natalie shouted just as Jesse walked into the room.

"Hey, hey. What's all the screaming about? Looks like everyone's fine to me," Jesse said to the three people he had never met.

Natalie turned to face him. "And who the hell are you? And what are you doing in my house?"

"He's the man in my dream," Daisy whispered quietly into Alfie's ear.

"Can we talk please, Natalie?" Jesse said, trying hard to take his eyes off the children as they both looked at him with new interest.

"Kids, stay here while I show this lunatic out and then we are going to have a talk about... about... well, we just need a talk," she said as she advanced towards Jesse, forcing him back onto the stairs and pulling the door closed behind her.

"I'm not sure I'm the lunatic," he said walking backwards down the stairs.

"And what's that supposed to mean?"

"Well, I'm not the one running around the garden in my nightclothes screaming for my children, am I?" he replied, the cheeky grin still on his face.

"Just get out of my house before I call the police."

"Natalie, please. I need to talk to you."

"And how do you know my name? Who the hell are you?"

Jesse suddenly came to a standstill, causing Natalie to almost walk straight into him.

"I'm a friend of Adam's," he said, "from the Brighton Sea Swimming Club."

"If you'd been a friend of Adam's, then I'd know you, wouldn't I?"

"Well, let's say I'm a new friend, then."

"Sorry, not possible, Adam's been dead five years. I'm calling the police."

"Even spirits need friends, Natalie. In some cases, they need friends more now than when they were alive."

With that, he turned around and walked down the last few stairs and across the large open hallway until he found the kitchen.

WHAT THE TIDE BRINGS BACK

"Let's have a cup of coffee and a chat," he said as he turned around from the kitchen entrance to look at her once again. "It's important, Natalie, we need to talk; your kids' lives could depend on the decision you take right now, so make the right one."

Daisy and Alfie had walked out of the gym and were looking down on them.

"Talk to him, Mum," Daisy called down.

"Get to your rooms, now," Natalie replied without looking up.

"He stopped Lilly getting me. He's my friend."

Natalie froze on the spot. She turned and looked up to see Daisy smiling down at her from the top of the stairs, before she shrugged and went back into the gym with Alfie, shutting the door behind her.

"Daisy, get out here. What the hell did you mean? How do you know about Lilly? Daisy…" Natalie screamed at her daughter.

"I don't understand it all myself, but something's happening to her, Natalie. Please, we need to talk."

Natalie looked at him and he could see her trying to decide on her next move.

"Please, give me a chance to explain," he added.

"The cups are in the cupboard above the microwave with the coffee. I take mine black, no sugar," Natalie said before turning around and walking back up the stairs heading to her bedroom to throw on some clothes.

CHAPTER NINETEEN

Marlene and James

Marlene pulled up outside 28 Goldstone Street, driving straight into a parking space. James was just coming to the door showing out his last patient of the day as Marlene pulled up.

"What the hell happened to your car?" he asked as he walked his patient to the pavement and stood next to the damaged bonnet.

"I lost concentration," she replied matter-of-factly.

"You're not wrong," he said, bending down to check out the damage to the radiator and the wings before standing back up and seeing the gash on her cheek. "I think you'd better come in," he said. "Let's get you cleaned up. How did you know where to find me?" he asked out of interest.

"Instinct," she replied sarcastically, causing him to shake his head as he led her into the surgery and sat her on the dentist chair as if she was going to have root canal treatment.

"Sit back and relax a minute; I just need to get some stuff."

"No drills or pliers, please," she said seriously.

"After the meeting at Jesse's this morning you'll be very lucky if I don't," he replied, smiling at her as he left the room.

James's surgery was a semi-detached converted house – the mirror image of the house next door where he lived with his family. As she sat back in the chair, Marlene glanced around the room, noticing the family photos. There were photos of James and his family either in their sailing boat at Brighton Marina or standing near the Brighton Palace Pier or swimming in one sea or another. Marlene wondered what it was that drove these people to spend so much time in such an inhospitable environment as the sea. To her, the sea meant cold. It meant danger; it even meant death now. Yet these people, these normal, sensible people, were drawn to it in a way that she could never fathom.

James came back into the small surgery followed by his wife, who worked as his dental nurse.

"Marlene, Jane – Jane, Marlene."

"Hi, Jane," Marlene offered.

Jane just smiled and put down the tray on the desk before giving James a peck on the cheek and heading out of the room.

"Don't be late back, I told you both the kids are coming for dinner. And lock up, will you," she said to him as she pulled the door shut.

"Sorry, I think perhaps I'm disturbing you," Marlene said, embarrassed suddenly being in this strange place with a virtual stranger.

"It's fine. It's me she's annoyed with, not you, she hates it when I move patients around as it takes her weeks to reschedule everyone."

Marlene replied guiltily, "I kind of forced you to come with me, didn't I? I'm sorry. And then how Jesse spoke to you – he was wrong to do that."

"Was that why you crashed the car? Did he chuck you out as well?" he asked as he dipped some cotton wool in a soothing ointment and started to dab it on her cheek.

She flinched as the cream immediately started to disinfect the area. "Yes, he pushed me away as well. I was so angry. I drove home too fast and, well, I missed a corner and drove straight through a fence."

Saying it out loud made her realise how crazy everything was starting to sound.

"And then what, you turned around and came right here to see a dentist? An odd decision," he said as he stepped back to find a plaster to cover the wound.

"I guess so!"

"Does Jesse know you're here?"

"Of course not. He might not want my help, but he needs it. And I think I need yours," she said.

"Stay still," James said as he held the plaster in both hands and then gently placed it across the wound before going back to his sink to rinse his hands. "Good as new; just leave it on for a couple of days and it'll be fine."

"Thanks," she said, grateful for the help but desperately wanting to get back to the subject of Jesse. "Will you help me, James? I can't do this on my own."

"Look, Marlene, if Jesse doesn't want our help then maybe we should just respect that."

Marlene sat forward on the chair and looked James square in the eye. "It's not just about him, though, is it? It's about Adam and Natalie's children as well. It's for their sake Jesse needs our help."

James sighed and rested himself back against the sink. "What can I do to help? I can't do all this mumbo jumbo psychic stuff you and Jesse do."

"I don't know what it is, but I can sense you know something, James, even about Lilly, maybe. There's something you're not telling me. I need to know what it is."

"I've told you everything I know."

"But have you, really?" Marlene challenged him.

James pushed himself to standing. "Yes," he said defiantly.

"OK, maybe I'm wrong then. I'm sorry, I thought you and the swimming club had history you could share. I'll leave you in peace," she said, turning to leave, hoping he would stop her.

He did.

"Actually, my family do go back about four generations in Brighton. Some of the original founders of the swimming club were my ancestors."

Marlene stopped and turned around, pleased that James had taken the bait.

"I don't suppose you have some old photos, or old family clippings from newspapers from those days, do you?" she pressed on, hoping to keep him engaged. "I think something happened in Brighton in the mid to late-eighteen hundreds, something that caused Lilly to lose her life. Maybe she just died here, in the city, or perhaps she was murdered. And it happened in or around the beach that your ancestors used to swim in. I've searched the local archives and the local papers for anything that might tie Lilly to the swimming club or the pier but couldn't see anything. There has to be something, though. Something that links Lilly to this, I'm certain of it. And something that links Lilly to the Austin family, something that only locals at the time would have been interested in. Maybe, your family kept something that will help us bring this all together without you even realising?"

Talking about his ancestors, especially being founders of the swimming club, was like a drug for James and he felt the adrenaline start to flow through his veins. "There may be something next door," he said, beckoning Marlene to follow him back out of the surgery, across the shared driveway and into his family home. He pushed the door open and walked with purpose past the kitchen and straight up the stairs. Marlene followed in his wake, trying to keep up with him. "I'm showing Marlene the family archives," James called out to Jane, not picking up her reply about the dinner being ready and being ruined if he took too long.

Marlene kept her head down as she passed the kitchen, understanding she was intruding in his personal life more than she wanted to.

"We keep all the old stuff in the spare room," he said as he

144

pushed open the first door on the right, flicking on the switch as he went in and lighting up the small eight by eight-foot box room with a light bulb that was as old as the papers that carpeted the floor and shone only a dim light on the contents. "The kids don't come back to stay much now, so I took back Jenny's room and put all the old stuff from the loft in here. I've started to organise it, you know, by date, subject, family member, that sort of thing. But it's a mammoth job; there must be over two hundred years of history in here. I've been at it for months and hardly made a dent in it all."

It was shocking for Marlene to see so much paper scattered everywhere. Apart from a small two-seater sofa, there was hardly space to put your foot down without treading on something over a hundred years old. She hoped that James had a system in here as otherwise this could take weeks, and they had days, if not hours at most.

"Can we narrow our search down a bit, James? Is there anything in here specifically about the seafront, or maybe the Austin Hotel? I don't suppose there's a photo showing a murder on the pier is there?" she said, joking, or at least half joking and half desperate.

"I don't know about any murders, but there's definitely something on the Austin Hotel; it was the fanciest hotel back in its day, it always got a lot of press. It's the Queens Hotel now. You wouldn't know by looking at it, but it was really something back then; absolutely magnificent. It's here somewhere," he said, carefully stepping between the scattered papers. Marlene was still in the doorway, not quite sure how to navigate her way into the room. "I think there was a bit about when it was sold, it was a huge shock to the seafront traders at the time."

James headed to the far corner, where the newspapers were piled as high as the window ledge and looked dangerously close to collapsing.

"I know it looks messy but it's actually much better than it was when it was all boxed in the loft; there was no order at all back then and a lot of it had already started to crumble away. Shame I had to get rid of so much. I've already put a lot of it into subject order and I was just starting to cross-reference it into dates and put them into protective files, but I haven't quite got there yet. It's an ongoing project, as you can see," he said, picking up a pile next to the wall and starting to flick through the old pages.

"I thought you said you had nothing that could help." Marlene bravely skirted around the edges of the room as James flicked through the files of papers. "I think you might have been holding back on me after all," she said with a smile in her voice.

"Well, I didn't really think about it when you first asked. When you told me about Lilly Baker and the Austin family, you never mentioned the seafront or the pier, did you? Here we are," he said, pulling a paper from the pile and sitting down on the old two-seater couch that sat with its back to the window and was conveniently only a single step away from where he was. Marlene trudged over to him, no longer trying the impossible of avoiding the carpet of news beneath her and sat next to him, looking over his shoulder as he carefully pulled the paper out of the protective see-through plastic file. "Front page – it must have been big news," he said.

The front page displayed a headline about the Austin Hotel. James passed the paper to Marlene.

"Careful with the pages, they're brittle," he said to her. She took the paper carefully and turned to the inside page. The article spoke of the tragedy for the Austin family in the great storm. "What does it say?" James asked.

Marlene read the article before summarising it for James. "It doesn't give a lot of facts, just that a storm forced the Chain Pier to part collapse and it says someone fell from the pier. They thought whoever it was could have been from the Austin Hotel as someone said they were wearing a uniform that looked like theirs.

It says that they tried to speak with the owner, a John Austin, but he was unavailable to comment."

Marlene carried on flicking through the papers but could find nothing more about the Austin Hotel, its owners or the person who lost their life. She handed the paper back to James and looked around her to see if there was another following paper on the pile next to her.

"Do you have the next one?" she asked desperately. "Maybe it names the person who died? That can't be the only article on the pier and the storm, or about someone's dying there, can it!"

"I remember seeing a paper dedicated to the old pier, it was maybe twenty-five or thirty years later, an anniversary piece, I think. But I don't remember anything in there about anyone who died. In fact, I don't really even remember reading that bit before."

He suddenly looked up at Marlene.

"Do you think the person who died was Lilly Baker?" he asked, suddenly drawn back to the story.

"I don't know," Marlene said. "She could have been at the hotel."

"But you said you thought she was murdered. This was an accident, wasn't it?"

"It certainly sounds like it," Marlene said. "But the time period fits and if it was Lilly then it ties her into the Austin family, doesn't it?"

Marlene stood up and headed to the door, old newspapers and photos crunching under her feet.

"I should go find Jesse."

"I'm not sure how much help I've been," he said.

"You've confirmed some things I was only guessing, that's a real help. You also patched me up rather well." Marlene placed her fingers over the plaster on her cheek. "Say sorry to Jane for disturbing your meal and I'll let you know what more I find out."

She headed down the stairs and out of the front door, the strength suddenly returning to her legs as she ran to her car with a new-found purpose.

CHAPTER TWENTY

Jesse

J esse was sitting at the breakfast bar sipping on a cup of steaming black coffee and swallowing a piece of banana bread that he had found in the bread bin by the kettle when Natalie walked into the kitchen.

She picked up the coffee that he had made for her.

"Please finish your breakfast, don't let me put you off," she said sarcastically.

Jesse wiped his mouth and dusted down the crumbs that he had dropped onto his faded red swimming club T-shirt.

"I hope you don't mind," he said, motioning to the slice of bread still in front of him. "But it's been a hell of a couple of days and I kind of forgot to eat."

"Sure, why not," she replied. "Break into my house, scare my children and then eat our breakfast, seems reasonable to me."

She took a sip of the coffee and pulled up a stool next to him.

"So, what's all this about?" Natalie asked, leaning forward and staring into Jesse's eyes. "You don't strike me as the type to break into someone's home and threaten them."

"Really?" Jesse smiled. "So what type am I, then?"

"I'd say you're an overconfident arsehole who thinks that a cheeky smile and sad teardrop birthmark will make any woman fall at his feet."

149

"Fall at his feet? That's a bit old-fashioned, isn't it?" he replied as he took a sip of his coffee.

"And I'd put money on it that there isn't a Mrs…"

"Daniels," he replied.

"Daniels. I bet there isn't, and never was, a Mrs Daniels waiting at home. So at what, mid-forties, and clearly overconfident, I'd say that puts you into arsehole territory."

"And you got that by watching me eat banana cake and drink coffee?" Jesse stared at her.

"So, tell me I'm wrong."

"Don't you want to know why I'm here?" he asked.

Natalie took another large gulp of her coffee, then pushed her chair back and got to her feet. "If you don't mind I think I'd prefer it if you'd just leave."

"Really, you don't want to know why I'm here?" he asked again.

"Perhaps, I'm a little curious, but no, I don't think so. I think it would be best if you left."

"You need me, Natalie."

Natalie laughed, but there was no humour in it. "Really, do I? Those lines might work on some other lonely women, but I am not one of them." She took another step closer to Jesse and spoke right at his face. "I don't know what you *think* you know about my husband, but whatever it is, it's too late. He's dead, OK. He killed himself in that fucking sea that you and your friends think is some heroic playground. Well, you can take it from me, it's not heroic, it's not brave, it's just stupid. If you all want to kill yourselves, then fine, kill yourselves, but don't for a minute think I care a goddam thing about you or any of them. Now please get out of my house." Natalie stood up and headed to the doorway expecting Jesse to follow her.

But he stayed seated at the breakfast bar.

"I said get out!" Natalie shouted at him, astonished that he had not moved an inch, but instead just sat, looking at her.

From out in the hall, Alfie and Daisy came running into the kitchen. Alfie stood in the entrance but Daisy ran straight over to Jesse and stood next to him.

"Daisy, come here," Natalie screamed.

Daisy looked up at Jesse and gave him a huge smile. "Thanks for helping me," she said to him.

"It's all right, tiger," he replied.

"Mum, Jesse's my friend."

"Who are you?" Natalie whispered to Jesse.

"Daisy, why don't you and your brother go play? Your mum and me have some things to talk about."

"Cool," she replied before walking back to Alfie, grabbing his arms and running back into the hall, dragging him with her.

"Natalie, we need to talk, this is serious."

"What the hell was that?" she said, turning to the now empty kitchen entrance then back to Jesse. "The last time I had a stranger in the house, the kids went crazy, and he was only delivering the groceries, and now here you are, calling my daughter tiger; only Adam ever called her that. And what did she mean you helped her? Who the hell are you?"

"It's complicated," he said, his eyes never leaving hers.

"Ten minutes," was all she said as she sat down at the kitchen table, a stony expression on her face.

"OK, then, I'll cut right to the chase. I don't believe for a second that your husband committed suicide. I think he went into the sea that morning to stop something from taking your children. He was lured into the storm and she took him."

"By something you mean someone, don't you? You're talking about Adam's *ghost.*"

She saw by Jesse's reaction that he had not expected her to respond like that.

"Yes, I know all about this mysterious ghost. It was all he talked about before…" she trailed off, shaking her head.

"He thought he could stop her, but she was waiting for him, she wanted him as well as your children. He could never have stopped Lilly, nor can you, and now she's back to finish off what she started. She wants your children, Natalie; she wants to take Alfie and Daisy to get revenge on someone or something that had to do with Adam and, like it or not, I'm the only one who can stop her."

"It was all in his head, there are no ghosts!" Natalie screamed at him, her frustration breaking through as the tears started to form.

"Then explain how I know all this? And explain my connection to Daisy."

"Yes, I'd like to understand how you two know each other. I'd like to know how a grown man, a stranger, knows my ten-year-old daughter!"

Jesse took in a breath; this was not going well and he knew this was going to sound even crazier, but he had no other way of saying it.

"She's been dreaming about Lilly, having nightmares. Lilly is trying to control her, make her do something. I was in one of her dreams. I made Lilly go away."

Jesse gulped back his now cold coffee in one go and put the cup down on the breakfast bar as if it was a full stop. He looked at Natalie and challenged her to answer.

Natalie stared back. Jesse had no idea what was coming next, but as each second passed, he felt more and more nervous that the reply she was building up to was not one he was going to like.

The empty coffee cup left Natalie's hand with the force of a tornado and, without Jesse's quick reactions, he would have ended up back in the hospital bed that he had slept in the night before.

"Get out, you freak, before I call the police!" Natalie screamed at him, causing the twins to come running back into the kitchen with startled looks on their faces.

With Daisy screaming at her to leave him alone, Natalie

literally chased Jesse out the house, slamming the front door on him as he headed down the stairs to the driveway.

★★★

Natalie slumped on the hallway rug, tears of anger and frustration streaming down her face. Alfie and Daisy, not knowing what else to do, joined in the crying and curled up to her as close as they could possibly get. It was the closest they had been to her in years, Natalie realised.

"I'm sorry, guys," she said, once she brought herself back in check. "I didn't mean to shout."

"Why did you do that, Mum?" Daisy asked.

"He wanted to talk about Daddy, that's all, and it upset me."

"Why did he want to talk about Dad?" Alfie asked.

"Why won't you ever talk about Dad?" Daisy added.

"Not now, guys, please. OK?"

The twins, no longer crying, looked at Natalie.

"I will, I promise, soon. It's just hard for me talking about him." They continued to look at her, saying nothing.

She held them tightly, not wanting to push them away ever again.

"OK, OK. Tonight, after dinner, we can snuggle on my bed; we haven't done that in ages, have we, and maybe we can pull out the photo books and talk about Dad, and we can cry as much as we all want to. What do you say?" she asked them, her stomach once again hosting the dance of the butterflies.

"OK," they said in unison.

"And maybe you can tell me about your dreams," she added, looking at Daisy.

Then in a flash, as only children can, the mood changed.

"Come on, Alfie," Daisy called as she grabbed his arm. "Let's go to the treehouse."

Natalie watched enviously as the twins switched from tears

and desperation to peace and laughter in the blink of an eye. She used to be able to do that. Adam used to be able to make her feel as though whatever the problem was it was easily dealt with, that nothing was ever really a problem. He used to make her feel so safe. But that was before he changed. Before he started disappearing down to the beach at any hour of the day or night. Before he started to become so secretive with her. Before the diary.

The diary. She hadn't thought about the diary for years. The last time she'd thought about it was when James had brought it to her after the coroner declared Adam's death a suicide.

"I found this in his swimming bag, I kept it hidden all along," James had told her after the police had closed the case.

"He always had it with him," she had said sadly. "He seemed more attached to that thing than he was to his own family."

"You need to read it, Natalie."

"Why didn't you give it to the police? It might have helped them." James had stared at the diary in his hands, seemingly not listening to Natalie. She remembered now that he had seemed almost fixated on it. He could barely let go of it as he tried to hand it to her. He became all *Lord of the Rings* about it. She'd expected him to start calling it his precious.

She'd never opened it, though. She'd taken it from him and had wrestled with needing to know what was in it and not wanting to see what had driven him to go into a crazy sea. Eventually, she had hidden it in a box in the loft, burying it under Adam's other personal stuff, hiding it away, never touching it again. It had been like a dark cloud continuously circling around her for the last five years, always in her mind, a secret she was scared to face but could not forget existed.

She walked up the two flights of stairs to the gym at the top of the house and went to the small loft at the back of the room. She knew exactly where the box was without even having to turn the light on.

She sat for the next half an hour on the floor of the gym with the box in her lap, not wanting to open it for fear of what she would find inside. But she had no choice, she needed to get the diary and tear it up, shred it, burn it. She put the box on the floor and opened the lid. Inside, she was faced with memories of the only man she had ever loved. His good watch, his cufflinks, his passport, photos, swimming goggles, Brighton Sea Swimming Club hat. She hadn't planned on keeping anything other than the photos and maybe the watch, but bit by bit she had found herself filling up the box with stuff that she could neither bear to face every day but equally could not bear to be without. The diary was in there as well. Right at the bottom, underneath all the memories.

She dug her hand into the box, reaching down to her elbow until she touched its leather sleeve. It took all her mental strength to drag her arm back, her fingers clinging onto the diary. She stared at it for minutes, desperate not to open it. She kidded herself that it was nothing, just notes that her husband felt he needed to record. Things that were personal to him that he didn't want anyone, even her, to see. What was wrong with that? Everyone was entitled to secrets, even from their partners. *We didn't have to share everything, did we?* she asked herself in her head. But she couldn't put it back now, not now it was in her hands. And she couldn't destroy it, not without looking at it. As much as she knew she shouldn't open it, she also knew that she had to. No one could just ignore the diary their partner kept. No one. Natalie certainly couldn't. She undid the string bow that had kept it sealed these last five years and carefully, almost reverently, pulled back its faded leather cover and turned to the first page.

June 10

   Hi, kids – Dad here! Yes, this diary is just for you, for when you've put me and Mum in an old folks' home – just to remind you that we were real people once with real hobbies and that maybe you could remember to visit us every now and again! Just joking, I'm sure you'd never do that to us, ha ha.

So here I am, sitting at my desk after my first day of cold-water swimming as a member of Brighton Sea Swimming Club, and my fingers are just about starting to feel the life come back into them; my feet, however, are still completely numb – luckily, I don't need my feet to write.

Maybe it's a midlife crisis thing, but I've now got a new hobby and am going to write it all down so that one day you guys can remember what a crazy brave nut your old man was.

So here we go, Day One

The temperature this morning apparently was still under fifteen degrees – I'm amazed at how quickly I acclimatised. I stayed in for about twenty minutes. I swam with James, my new swimming buddy. There were about ten others out there with us, I don't know their names yet. James went all the way around the pier but I bottled out near the end – only just, though. It was so lovely out there and the others were egging me on; next time I'll go all the way around with them; what is a man to do?

Day Two

I got all the way to the end of the pier today, which was the furthest out I've ever been in the sea, but then I got the willies and bottled it, letting James and the others go around the whole pier without me. My heart started beating like a snare drum and I started to hyperventilate. I hid it from the others, of course, as I didn't want to spoil their swim, which was probably a bit silly. Perhaps a bit of male pride getting in the way of safety. I let them head off and then I turned back. I got back to shore pretty quickly, though; the sea was flat and the few waves that did come along seemed happy to let me bodysurf back in. When I got to standing depth, I felt a little silly at how I reacted, so I hung about a bit,

*floating on my back, and waited for the others to come back around,
which they did about ten minutes later. I would guess perhaps it
took them no more than twenty minutes to go all the way around;
they have a decent pace.*

*Considering it was so early in the morning and still quite dark,
it was funny to see fishermen out so early; I never realised they still
used little rowing boats. There were maybe three of them out there
in all; apparently at this time of year the mackerel are in abundance
around the pier (though lobsters and langoustines would suit me
better!) and the fishing boats (just some little rowing boats, really)
are on the hunt. There was one particular one that caught my eye
as there seemed to be a lady on her own in it; can you imagine
Mummy out in a little rowboat in the morning trying to catch us
breakfast, ha!*

Day Three

*A late write-up today, kids. I did swim at 7am but I was a
little spooked and I didn't fancy writing about it until now – looks
like your dad is not super dad after all, sorry to break it to you!*

*It's nine at night now and you two are in bed at last. Daisy,
you really played up tonight, tiger, and Mummy is still busy doing
playroom tidying duty because you two are so messy :0)*

*I'm sitting here wondering on the craziness of being so very
scared of something, especially at my age; perhaps crazy is an odd
word to use, but it does feel a bit crazy in the cold light of day. When
you are in a spooky building your mind makes up all kinds of crazy
stuff like ghosts, ghouls and monsters, but when you're swimming
in the sea and you start to hear noises, the ghosts and ghouls become
sea monsters, sharks, dead sailors coming back from the deep –
what your mind says is floating beneath you suddenly feels very
real indeed. When you eventually get to solid ground it all seems so
silly. The bells you hear ringing under the water and the rotting,
sea-bitten hands grabbing your ankles and dragging you under the*

waves are in reality just the rattle of the chains on the buoys attached to the seabed every few hundred metres, and the hands are just pieces of seaweed floating around you and twisting around your ankles. At the precise moment it's happening, deep down in your conscious mind you know it's the buoys and the seaweed, but your subconscious, your make-believe mind, screams sunken ships and dead sailors, swim for your life!

This morning I did manage to get around the whole pier with James, the first time I've braved the whole swim. It was just the two of us today as the others swam towards the burnt-out shell of the West Pier. James suggested we go with them as I hadn't done the West Pier swim before and if we stayed close to the shore the whole way it would be safe, but I wanted to go around the pier; truth be known, I almost felt I had to swim around it – maybe again that whole man thing of I won't be beaten this time. We swam up the side of the pier, staying quite close to give me some comfort, and went anti-clockwise around it. It was fine to begin with, uneventful and even invigorating. With the sea almost glass-like and definitely a bit warmer than the last few days, I felt I was back in the pool (apart from the cold, of course) and I swam fast. I think I surprised James as I had to wait for him at the end of the pier to let him catch me up; pool swimmers may not like the cold, but we can be super-fast after all those years of drills trained into us! Being at the end of the pier was amazing. Looking up, I could see the back of the rollercoaster just hanging there, almost suspended in mid-air and ready to fall over the end of the pier. There was also some music coming out from somewhere on the pier – and a lovely smell. I couldn't work out what it was at first but it seemed to tickle my throat and it even made me want to cough. It brought back a memory, something that I couldn't quite recall at that moment, a perfume I'd tasted before somewhere.

Up to then all was good and I was fantastically pleased to have made it that far without getting into a cold panic again.

It didn't last, though! As soon as James caught up with me, we had a little chat about the sunrise before heading back. The music was turned off by then and the strange smell had wafted away, so we carried on around and headed back down the other side of the pier back to shore. Halfway back, there are some stairs that lead from the pier down to the sea – a landing area for maintenance people, I guess – and then it was a short swim under the pier back to our own side, and back in. All seemed doable and surprisingly unchallenging by the time I reached the stairs. Coming under the pier, though, I heard bells ringing and they stopped me dead in my tracks, mid-stroke in fact. James went flying past without stopping and my heart jumped a gear. It was then that the seaweed took hold of my ankles and I had this insane fear of a hand dragging me down to hear the ringing bells, Quasimodo of the sea! I literally jumped out of my skin, if jumping while in the middle of the sea is even possible! My reaction was way over the top – it's embarrassing now. By the way, kids, I am NOT like that in real life, please remember that when reading this. Or at least I don't think I am!

Anyway, I got swimming again as fast as I could and literally raced myself to the beach; I shot past James near the shore and almost leapt out onto the stones like a madman. I think I worried him a little as I rushed onto the beach and sat down for a second to compose myself. If it hadn't been for that perfume smell hitting me again as soon as I reached the shore, I swear I would have sunk to my knees and cried; it was only there for a split second but it really soothed me, hypnotic even. I think I need to check out Mummy's perfume collection as maybe it's one she wears – why it was at the beach, I have no idea. Maybe it was just stuck in my nose?

I admitted to James later, after we had showered, how scared I had really been. He said it was all in my mind and that he'd had the fear loads of times over the years himself; apparently, all of them have it at times.

He said that there were some footings from the old Chain Pier still out there and on a very low tide you could see them buried in the sea floor. He said he hates swimming over them and every time he goes near them his heart starts to race and his swimming speed slows right down as he tries to speed up and loses all coordination. I guess not being able to see what's underneath you could spook anyone.

Anyhow, let's just say for now that it spooked me enough to stop me writing this morning, but not enough to stop me going back tomorrow for day four of my new hobby.

Day whatever – I've lost count already!

Writing what I am about to write is weird; in fact, keeping a diary at all still feels kind of weird – I hope you guys appreciate all this effort I am making for you! The truth is I actually feel I need to write this down, not just for you guys, but because I simply can't make sense of it otherwise. Kids, if you read this in fifty years' time, please don't think your old man was crazy! I drove to the beach as usual this morning and parked up near the pier again. Usually, I see a handful of runners, even at that time of the morning, and today was no exception as there were about a dozen of them in the first ten minutes. But this morning, I also saw that girl, that one from the fishing boat I noticed a few days ago. I know I only glanced briefly at her the other day and she was some distance away, but it was definitely her again this morning. She was standing on the promenade right by the entrance to the pier. I noticed her as soon as I got out of the car. She was staring at me; it felt like she was locking eyes with me. In the seconds it took me to grab my bag and lock my car, she was gone. What's that about? If I was an artist, which I'm not, I could draw her right now, every single detail; maybe I should ask Mummy to do it for me, she could do it for sure. I don't know how in that brief moment I remembered so much, but I bet if I think back a couple of days to having seen her in the fishing boat I could have done the same even then. Let's see if I can do this for you – she is about five foot seven inches, slim bordering on skinny, and stunning in that way that some people just are even if it's not exactly obvious why they are. Her hair is strawberry blonde – a very natural colour, I'd say – and it hung down her neck over her shoulders. Her eyes, which really are what grab you about her, are pale blue. I've never seen such a pale blue in eyes before, even bluer than mine, and it's amazing how on a darkish morning, standing about thirty feet away from me, I could see them so clearly. And her clothes were really odd… old, in fact. Not damaged old, just old, old, like age-old, costume-hire shop old. She had on a long dress that was off-white, cotton perhaps, with red velvet around the edges, frilly in places and neck to toe. I literally ran to the spot where she was standing. It was only about thirty feet from my car and a few steps away, but she wasn't there! By the time I got my wits about me, the runners were long gone as well, so I couldn't even stop and ask them where she went. It was the way she locked eyes with me, though, as if she knew me. It was definitely the girl from the boat, definitely, I'd swear my life on it.

Day Seven

I woke up to that perfume smell again this morning, the one from the beach, it made me cough myself awake. All four of us were in our bed (as usual). We all woke up together at 6:30am, you probably won't remember (!), but only I was coughing. What's weird is that it made me think of that girl I saw at the pier again. Why it would make me think of her, I have no idea.

I've been thinking that I might not do this sea swimming much longer – maybe just a couple more days to finish the week. I think I might miss sea swimming a little and I'll miss some of the people there, James is a good bloke, and the others are all pretty nice as well, but it's becoming an obsession now, I think; even your mum is starting to suggest I should stop, as it's apparently 'all I talk about'. How did a week in the sea take over my life so quickly? I spoke to the guys at the beach this morning before we went in the sea and they think I'm hooked and will keep coming back; they can see it in my face, apparently. How wrong they are. I will stop at the end of the week. I have nothing more to write today.

Day Eight
Today's swim was completely different from yesterday. Yesterday it was calm and flat, today it was rough and bumpy, so much so that we could hardly get in. Six of us this morning were standing at the edge of the beach in a really strong wind trying to force our way into a very angry sea. I'm a little too new at this to just go diving in, so I let the other more experienced ones give it a go; three got in and two didn't. The ones who got in tried to come straight out and almost didn't make it; I was certainly pleased not to be the brave one. So, instead, we did an odd thing; we all lay down on the stones like pilchards and let the waves roll over us. Apparently, it's normal to do this, although in whose world this is deemed normal I am not entirely sure. Without wishing to sound crazy, it was rather invigorating. So my last day but one I did not actually get to swim in the sea. Tomorrow I'll take a camera with me as otherwise I am sure you will think I am making it all up.

The door to the gym burst open, bringing Natalie back to the present.

"Mum, is dinner ready yet?" Daisy asked.

"Are you crying again, Mum?" Alfie ran to her and pulled her face up.

"Oh my goodness, look at the time," Natalie said to them. "Why didn't you call me before now, you must be starving?"

"We were playing. Is dinner ready yet?"

"Why are you crying, Mum?"

Natalie pulled Alfie close and let Daisy come and join in.

"Sorry, guys, it's been a strange day, hasn't it? I've been looking at photos of Dad. The man from this morning made me realise I'd forgotten what having Dad around was like and I think it has just made me sad."

"Shall we make dinner, Mum?" Daisy asked, suddenly all grown up.

"It's OK, munchkin, I'm on it. Tell you what, let's pop out and grab a takeaway or something, it's too late to start cooking now."

"Burger King!" shouted Alfie.

"McDonalds chicken!" shouted Daisy.

"Burger King's closest. We'll eat there and then come home and snuggle up and look at Dad's photos like I promised, what do you say?"

"Yay, Mum, you're the best."

"Woo hoo!" cried Alfie as he and Daisy pulled at Natalie's arms and dragged her to the door. The diary fell off Natalie's lap and landed back in the box. As she and the kids headed down the stairs, a familiar smell hit her nose and caused a cough to form in the back of her throat. She decided it must have come from the box, maybe even the diary; old stuff often carried smells from the past in them.

Once they got back home from dinner, all three of them got straight into their nightclothes and jumped into Natalie's bed. They spent the next two hours pouring over everything that Natalie had brought down from the gym – all the old photos of her and Adam from their wedding nearly twenty years before, the baby photos from ten years ago and more family holidays than she even remembered them taking. By the end of the evening, the twins were wrapped up in Adam's old shirts, his smell still lingering on them, and Alfie was sporting his watch while Daisy was holding one of his cufflinks tightly in her hand not ready to ever let it go. It was past ten o'clock when Natalie finally led the twins half asleep back to their own room.

After she had settled them both, she turned the light down very low and stood watching them for another five minutes. This day had long been coming and she knew that it was for the best, the three of them bringing Adam out from the dark and back into their lives.

"I should have done it before tonight, guys, I know that now," she whispered to them as they slept. "But I just wasn't ready. But we mustn't forget Daddy, we must never forget him. I'll make sure we don't. Sleep well; tomorrow will be a better day, I promise. Tomorrow we'll start being a family again."

Natalie went straight from the twins' room back up the stairs to the loft and scooped up the diary. As she walked back down to her bedroom, she felt herself caressing the leather cover and understanding what Adam had meant when he said it felt so old and comforting; it was almost as if the diary wanted to share its story with her. She climbed back into her bed and opened it where she had left off. She was no longer tired, ten o'clock suddenly felt like five o'clock again. She was hungry for its story, desperate to embrace her husband again, and she needed to start doing that right away.

CHAPTER TWENTY-ONE

Jesse

After leaving Natalie's house, Jesse cycled back home, frustrated. He wasn't sure exactly what he'd expected to happen, but it certainly wasn't that. The bike ride took him no more than twenty-five minutes and he arrived anxious. Anxiety was not an emotion Jesse usually felt. Anger, resentment, curiosity and, when in the sea, even peace and comfort; these were the emotions that fed him, but anxiety was a new one and not one he enjoyed. Natalie had stirred feelings in him that he had never known he had. Amongst the shouting and throwing of cups, he somehow felt himself physically attracted to her; it was not the reaction he had expected. He'd no idea what she would look like before he arrived there; somehow in his head he thought he'd find a broken down, weak and vulnerable woman; characteristics that he found most unattractive. He had never expected to meet by far the most stunning woman he had ever seen. And it was more than just the physical. Natalie was the whole package, beautiful on the outside and clearly passionate and intelligent in equal measures. For the first time in his forty-two years, Jesse felt the stirrings of something within his heart; something he did not possess the skills to understand.

He parked his bike outside his house and tried to shake the feeling. He had no time for love in his life; it was too complicated; it meant sharing. He'd watched enough TV and read enough books to know that love meant giving oneself up to one's partner. Jesse knew he could never do that; he could never share his feelings – he didn't even understand them himself, it would be impossible to bring someone else into them, especially someone who had a family as well; impossible. But she seemed so perfect, so beautiful. He tried to put Natalie to the back of his mind as he opened the front door.

Before Jesse was even through the door, Susie was standing on the landing, her face full of thunder.

"Easy, Susie," he said, backing up to the door.

"Where have you been, Jesse?" she screamed at him. "You just vanished again. You could have called me, you never texted or anything. You can't just turn up and expect to sleep with me when you want and then just leave." The anger turned to tears as the frustration overwhelmed her.

"Susie, I'm sorry, it's just not a great time…"

"Jesse…" she said softly between the tears. "Why do you have to be this way?"

He said nothing. He stepped forward, took her in his arms and pulled her in close. He needed her now, more than ever. He needed to clear Natalie from his head. And Lilly. And Marlene. In fact, everyone.

Jesse was exhausted by the time Susie fell asleep. The sex had been furious. They both seemed to have a point to make. The moment after they had stumbled into her flat they fell through the bedroom door and clawed at each other's clothes. Jesse's time with Susie could never be described as lovemaking, it was often brutal and exhausting; exactly the company he had needed. But now that she was fast asleep, he was suddenly overwhelmed with a feeling of extreme loneliness. It hit him so unexpectedly that tears formed in his eyes and started to run down his cheeks. It was another emotion Jesse was not used to and it shook him.

Throughout his life, Jesse had used people and people had

used him; it was an arrangement that suited him perfectly, as it meant he never had to share or even acknowledge his feelings, so the sudden feelings that swamped him now made no sense. Was it Natalie? Had she stirred something in him that had been sitting dormant for years ready to be woken? Was it Marlene and the way she tried constantly to make him feel needed and worthy and part of a family? Or was it Lilly Baker? Jesse sat bolt upright, forcing Susie to move over to her side of the bed in her sleep. Was it Lilly's feelings that were now coursing through his body and mind? Marlene had told him that the next stage of his gift would likely come to him unexpectedly, at a time when he was focused deeply on something else, and Susie had certainly kept him focused for the last two hours. He lay back on the pillow and tried to close down the thoughts in the left side of his brain and concentrate on the right – the creative side, the side which Marlene said controlled his gift.

Marlene and he had spent numerous hours and done numerous exercises on engaging the right side of the brain and closing down the left, she was constantly telling him to use instinct instead of reason and to just trust rather than question. But it was so hard to stop questioning everything. Every time he thought about it and tried to use instinct alone, he would find his brain trying to throw in reason and logic. He lay back on the pillow, closed his eyes and took some deep breaths. In and out, in and out, filling his lungs with oxygen and exhaling as quietly but as fully as his exhausted body would allow him to. Within minutes, his eyes started to close. He tried to keep breathing deeply and exhaling rhythmically, but bit by bit sleep took him over and he had no choice but to succumb.

As he drifted off to sleep, he felt arms wrapping themselves around him. He tried to open his eyes, but they felt like lead weights had been attached. He could hear Susie whispering into his ear and feel her soft kisses as they traced down from his forehead, over his eyes, reaching his mouth, her lips forcing his mouth open as her tongue delved deep inside, searching around, finding his own. He tried to respond but he couldn't move, couldn't react. A perfume filled the room and crept down his open mouth, deep down into his lungs, choking him, making him want to cough, but he couldn't.

"John, don't fight me. Love me, John. Take me." The voice was sweet, calming. It wasn't Susie's. "Love me, John, love me like I love you."

"I do love you, Lilly. I love you so very much."

The words came from his mouth, but they weren't his words. He could feel himself becoming aroused and he could feel her on top of him, taking him deep inside her. And he felt that a part of him loved her, wanted her so badly. But it wasn't him, he was a stranger to himself.

He felt her breath as she continued to kiss him, harder and harder, his lungs burning as he tried to breathe out the perfume that was invading his body. But she held him so tightly that he couldn't move her. And his body responded, but he had no control over it.

"Now, John, now!" he heard her screaming into his head.

★★★

Suddenly, Jesse was awake. But he wasn't in bed. He wasn't himself. He wasn't where he should have been.

He was at the Old Steine in the heart of Brighton's bustling seafront. It was a beautiful sunny Sunday morning and across the road he could see the Chain Pier swaying slightly in the morning breeze. The crowds had flocked to walk over it and gaze down at the sea below and the whole seafront was buzzing with the energy of a new morning. Jesse stumbled backwards against the railings next to the fishing nets. The smells and sights of the unfamiliar surroundings made him giddy. He knew this was Brighton seafront, but this was not the Brighton he was used to. And the people around him were dressed in clothes that would not look out of place in a museum. To Jesse they were ludicrous. Men in top hats and long jackets, and women in long dresses covering almost every inch of their skin. Yet, there was also something comforting about them; there was a part of him that felt at home standing there. He knew without looking down at himself that he was also dressed in a tailored suit and on his head, proud and brushed, stood a hat as tall and elegant as any parading before him.

Something felt different physically as well. He felt taller, and fuller. Not fat, just fuller around the waist. He looked down and saw himself – dressed differently for sure, but still the same Jesse; forty-two years old and greying at the temples, five foot ten inches, lean, broad swimmer's shoulders and muscles in all the right places. But he didn't feel like that. He felt younger, still in his mid-thirties, his muscles were weighty as if covered with layers of fat that he had never had, he felt at least three inches taller, but his shoulders felt rounded, as if he had a very minor stoop. He tried to straighten up, but the urge to lean forward overrode this and he had no choice but to let his body do whatever it needed to do.

"Excuse me, guvnor, do you mind moving yerself."

Jesse turned to see a man gathering up some fishing nets he'd left to dry the evening before, ready for the morning's early start. The fishermen all gathered here on Sundays to tend their nets, not only to be ready for the next day's catch but also because it was a tradition that had formed over the years and fishermen were, if nothing else, sticklers for tradition.

"Sorry, I didn't realise it was you, sir," he said to Jesse as he turned to face him.

"Do you need a hand with your nets?" Jesse found himself asking as if he had known the man for years.

"Just unhook it there, if you don't mind, much appreciated," he said, gesturing to his net that was caught on the railings. "Are you hoping for anything special from tomorrow's catch, Mr Austin?"

Jesse answered him without hesitation, it felt natural to do so. "Just the usual catch would be perfect. We're full at the moment and I'm expecting the hotel to be busy all weekend."

The fisherman carried on talking, but Jesse's focus changed, as he was suddenly aware of someone looking at him. She was standing over the road, her eyes boring into his, not leaving him even for a second. Despite the crowds and the general excitement of the area, Jesse sensed her the moment she arrived. She was smiling at him and he couldn't help but smile back. He watched as she moved towards him through the crowds and carefully weaved her way across the road between the horses and carriages.

"Is it not enough that you run the finest hotel on the seafront, Mr Austin? Now, you have to teach the fishermen how to gather their nets as well," she commented dryly.

It took all Jesse's willpower not to grab her tightly around the waist and pull her to him. Her perfume surrounded him, sickly sweet on anyone else but sunny and fresh on Lilly. Despite that, though, it still caught in his throat, causing him to cough.

"Are you going to kiss me, then, Mr Austin?" she teased.

Jesse grabbed her roughly by the wrist, as an angry parent would a naughty child, and pulled her away from the glaring eyes of the fishermen into a shadowy corner around the side of the Austin Hotel that backed onto the Old Steine. With no one able to see them, he kissed her firmly on the mouth. Her tongue found his hungrily as he pulled her in deeper and deeper. Feeling his manhood pushing against her, Lilly quickly pulled herself away and looked around to be sure no one was near.

"Not here, John, not like this. What if we're seen?"

"When?" Jesse asked, breathless with desire, her perfume bathing him in its flowers.

"We have to be careful; if Mary catches us…"

"My wife's working front of house tonight, she'll be at the desk until the morning."

"Back at the hotel then, tonight. I'll find you," she said, pulling away and smoothing her dress.

Pushing Jesse away, she moved out of the shadows and back across the busy road, almost getting caught under the hooves of a very excitable mare. Jesse ran after her as she headed west along the seafront towards the North Laines. He had to work hard to keep up with her as his body felt clumsy and unfamiliar. They reached the entrance to the Laines in under ten minutes, Lilly seeming full of energy while Jesse was out of breath and bent double.

"Come on, old man," Lilly teased him. "Can't you keep up?"

Lilly hurried past the numerous stalls lining the road selling everything from food and drink to household goods and stopped at one selling arts and crafts. After a few minutes of haggling about price and testing the quality, she handed Jesse a beautiful, handmade leather-bound diary and a set of hand-carved pencils. He noticed the stall was called Bower & Sons.

A memory surfaced. He was in the Laines with Marlene in an old bookshop – the name Bower & Sons proudly displayed over the door.

Lilly sensed his internal battle.

"Go away!" her voiced screamed into his head. "Go away, I want John, not you, I want John!"

The memory vanished and he felt her putting the diary and pencils into his hands and kissing him softly on the cheek. He smiled.

"Now you have no excuses," she said. "I want to hear no more about why you can't find the time to write. It's all you talk about, John Austin. If you didn't have the hotel taking up your time you would write love poems just for me. So now you've no excuse, have you? Every night when the guests are in their rooms and Mary is asleep next to you, I expect to see a candle burning down the hall so I can picture you writing all the things you think about us doing together."

"You expect me to do that in front of Mary?" Jesse asked, knowing instinctively that Mary Austin was his wife. He felt a deep love for Mary Austin at that moment.

"Expect it? I insist on it," Lilly said, leading the way straight back to the seafront and the hotel.

Jesse stood outside, looking up at what he vaguely recognised as the Queens Hotel, directly in front of the Brighton Palace Pier. But this was not the Queens and the Palace Pier was not where it should be. He felt Lilly in his mind again, forcing him out, bringing John back in.

The sign across the front entrance shone out; Austin Hotel. It was an imposing building, ten storeys high, with balconies across its face giving the impression of open eyes looking out to sea. It stood alone with its modern frontage, almost daring its monolithic neighbours to look on it with envy. The entrance door was circular and set on a turntable, the first of its kind in the town, and it welcomed guests directly into a grand hall and reception area where the manager greeted them.

"Afternoon, Mr Austin," he said, turning his back on Lilly. "Afternoon, Bradley," Jesse said to his longest-serving employee.

"Are you feeling all right, sir?" Bradley asked him as Jesse felt the colour draining from his face.

"Yes, Bradley, I'm fine, just fine," Jesse managed to get out, his voice deeper and his accent more clipped than he was used to.

"Would you like tea in the Markwell lounge, sir?" Bradley suggested.

"Perhaps I will take tea in my room – I am a little tired," Jesse replied. "Lilly, please bring me some tea up."

"Miss Lilly will be expected by Mrs Austin any time now, sir," said Bradley, giving Lilly a ferocious look. "I will send tea to your room right away, sir."

"Miss Lilly…" Lilly repeated in the over-English tone of Mr Bradley, "is fully aware of her duties, thank you, Mr Bradley, and I will find Mrs Austin as soon as I have served tea to Mr Austin. Now please go about your business and I shall go about mine," she finished with a threatening look.

Mr Bradley, clearly furious at being spoken to like that by the chambermaid, stormed off.

"Lilly, you shouldn't," Jesse said. "We need to be discreet."

"Miserable old goat," Lilly whispered to Jesse, as they walked past. "He hates me. You should sack him. Anyway, we are discreet. No one knows, do they?" she whispered.

"If Mary found out…"

"She won't. Go to your room, I'll find Mary and then I'll come up."

When Lilly eventually came to the room, she took the diary from Jesse's hands, stroking it almost reverently, as if it were the most precious thing she had ever held in her life.

"Look after this, John," she said. "Always carry it with you – you never know; one day, I might even want you to write my own life story in it – a rags to riches tale of a future hotelier."

She kissed the diary gently on its brown leather cover and put it down. Taking Jesse's hand, she kissed it and led him to the bed. Whatever innocence Lilly's face portrayed was abandoned in the bedroom.

***

Jesse couldn't breathe. Gasping, his hands went instinctively to his throat. Someone's hands were wrapped tightly around his neck. His eyes shot open in shock. Susie was lying on top of him, mid-intercourse, with her hands choking the life out of him.

He tried to relieve the pressure on his neck, to stop her, but her grip was too strong. The more he tried to pull them off, the harder her grip became. He tried desperately to unlock himself from her hips, to pull himself out of her, but the more he tried the heavier she became, her hips pushing down harder and harder, drawing him deeper and deeper into her. She climaxed with an animal fierceness, a scream that flooded the silence of the room.

Jesse tried to draw in a breath, to stop himself losing consciousness. He couldn't understand what was happening. He looked up into Susie's face and saw the pain she was in, but her eyes, they looked at him with a hatred he had never seen in her before. And they looked at him with the same blueness that only one other person possessed. He suddenly understood.

Gathering his last breath and with every ounce of strength left in him he bucked his hips, throwing Susie to the left, and rolled away from her, tumbling out of bed onto the floor. Stale air suddenly filled his lungs and the sweat poured off him.

"You almost killed me," he croaked to her.

"What's happening?!" she looked to him, fear etched all over her face. "What happened? Look at me, Jesse, look at me!" she screamed.

He stood up and looked at her on the bed, seeing the bruises all around her thighs, all the way down her legs.

"I couldn't stop, I wanted to stop, but couldn't," she cried. "You were calling me Lilly, I could hear it in my head, you were calling me Lilly and saying you loved me. Who's Lilly, Jesse? Who the fuck's Lilly? Why couldn't I stop?"

Tears streamed down Susie's face as she fell back onto the bed, terrified and bewildered.

"Susie, I… it… it wasn't me. You were strangling me, I couldn't breathe. Oh God, what did she do to us?"

"She?" Susie looked up at him. "What's happening, Jesse? What's going on?"

"I'm sorry, I'm so sorry."

"Jesse…"

He looked at the clock. It was four in the morning. He started to pull on his clothes as Susie continued to stare at him.

"You can't just leave." Her voice broke as tears overcame her. Gasping, she said, "Jesse, you can't just leave like that. Who is she, Jesse? Who is…" As he reached the front door, he noticed Susie's car keys on the sideboard. He stopped for a second to get his breath back and to pull his T-shirt over his head. He looked down at the keys and then back to the door where Susie's voice was still trying to wake up the neighbourhood.

"Sorry, Susie," he whispered into the darkness. "I don't suppose you mind me borrowing your car, do you?" he said as he scooped the keys and headed out the door.

Susie's new white BMW Sport was parked in its usual spot in the private bay directly outside the front door. Within minutes, Jesse was speeding along the A23 heading out of Brighton towards Hurstpierpoint.

He pulled up outside Marlene's house just fifteen minutes later, having broken every speed limit going. He clambered out of the car, desperate to talk to her. He stopped at the door, unsure what he was going to say. He couldn't call it a dream, it was anything but a dream, it was as real as him standing there now. He had been there. He had met Lilly in the flesh. In fact, he had more than met Lilly, he realised, feeling hot and flustered again.

And she had almost killed him, again. He also now knew how Adam and Natalie Austin were tied into all this; Adam had to be a descendant of John Austin, Lilly's lover. What he didn't yet know was what happened between Lilly and John over a hundred years ago that caused her to come back now and take Adam's life, knowing that it was the key to saving Adam and Natalie's twins from the same fate.

Jesse took a deep breath and rang the doorbell. There was no reply, so he rang again. After three tries, he was about to bang on the door with his fists when the door flew open. Marlene stood there in her dressing gown and slippers, a worried look etched on her face.

"We need to talk," Jesse said as he pushed past her into the lounge and on into her kitchen. "Coffee?" he called out as he picked up the kettle.

"It's four in the morning," Marlene pleaded.

"Is it? Black or white?"

"What?"

"The coffee, black or white?"

"White," Marlene said, shaking her head as she sank into her comfort chair in the lounge and switched on the lamp next to her.

"He's your son, you tell him," she said to Jesse's father as she yawned.

"What was that?" Jesse called from the kitchen.

"Just telling your dad that you are impossible," Marlene replied.

"Oh, right," Jesse said.

He came back into the room and set the cup in front of her before taking the chair opposite.

"What's so important it couldn't wait until morning?" she asked.

"It is morning. And I slept with Lilly. Or at least John Austin did; well, I guess we both did. Oh, and she tried to get Susie to kill me."

Marlene sat back in her chair, totally lost for words.

CHAPTER TWENTY-TWO

Natalie

N atalie closed the diary and looked at the clock next to her bed. It was just turning four o'clock in the morning. She felt as if she knew more about Adam now than when he had been alive. She had never wanted to hear about the sea, it had frightened her so much – the tides, the waves, everything about it scared her. She had been petrified he would go out one day and never come back; it turned out she had been right to worry.

The sea swimming had taken hold of him in a way that she could never understand, but at least now, having read about so many days in his diary, she could at least get a feeling as to why he did it. Day after day, he had written about the people he swam with, about the arch they swam from, the amazing sunrises and the crazy storms; the days they swam around the pier to the days that the sea kept them out and they lay on the beach like pilchards or stood at the end of the groin waiting for a sea shower. He had been particularly proud of the days he had swum around the pier in under ten degrees Celsius, and the madness of swimming in deep winter when the snow fell onto the beach and settled up past his ankles. But always in there, in between those normal days, he mentioned *her*. Not every day, but as the diary went on, week by week and month by month, it became more noticeable. And his writing became more erratic. He went from writing in the diary to the children to writing to the diary as if it were itself a living

177

thing that was waiting to be fed. Page by page, she could feel his personality changing, just as she had week by week when he was alive, only then she was living with it and not understanding it; but now, she was finally beginning to understand. She looked at the clock one last time, desperate for sleep. She was so tired but she just couldn't put the diary down. There was more she needed to know. It held secrets that Adam should have shared with her, and it was time he gave them up.

She turned the page and read on.

I know her name now, it's Lilly Baker. Or at least in my dream that was her name. I hardly ever remember my dreams – in fact, when Natalie regales me with her dreams of finding herself in someone's home but it's not their home, and I am there but it's not me and all that nonsense, I sit there wondering why I never remember anything, why my dreams always escape me. This morning, though, I remembered everything; her name, her expressions and even her perfume. I told Natalie about it over breakfast and she said it was the first time I'd ever told her about a dream I'd had; she also wanted to know who Lilly was. It seems I was quite animated when describing her.

Natalie thought back to that day. It was years ago now, but the memory of it came right back to her as if it had happened just this morning.

"How do you know her name was Lilly when you say you've never spoken to her?"

"I don't know. I just know."

"Well, that's silly."

"Really! Well, coming from Mrs Dream-a-lot-of-nonsense I'll take that as a compliment – I think."

Natalie smiled as she remembered. She carried on reading.

I woke up exhausted this morning, sweating and with the noise from outside our bedroom window ringing in my ears.

I didn't want to be awake, I wanted to stay with Lilly. I wanted to find out who she really was; and why I suddenly knew her name. But I was awake and I was back in the real world; the world of work, family and the twenty-first-century racket.

For the first time since they were born, I resented the kids jumping on me and waking me up, and I think they felt it. In fact, I know they felt it. I tried to smile at them but I think it was a scowl as Alfie moved away from me and snuggled into Nat. Even Daisy, my little tiger, slid a little away from me, and my tiger never does that.

Why is it, though, that four hours later and sitting at my desk, I am still in a bad mood when it was only a dream? Lilly Baker, figment of my imagination or not, you have put me in a bad mood today and I do not much appreciate it.

Annoyingly, really annoyingly, I couldn't even remember what the dream was about, just the fact that it made me unhappy. I left the house at my usual half-six, without waking my brood, or upsetting them. I was dismayed as it was windy again and had hoped for a decent swim, perhaps even around the pier a couple of times. Luckily, when I got to the beach, I found that the wind had only stirred the sea up a little and the general consensus was that a pier swim was actually doable. So we went in. The waves were looking very big to me but I thought, what the hell, may as well go for it, just needed to make sure I didn't tell Natalie.

We headed off around the pier. I made sure I stayed close to James so that neither of us was alone, and we trailed slightly behind Sarah, Bob and Geoff, who it seems have no fear at all. We stopped for a brief and very bumpy chat at the end of the pier; even with the waves jostling us around, it seemed to be the thing to do. Although it was disconcerting looking back to the shore half a mile away, by watching walls of water heading in at speed we knew that we would soon be right in the middle of them. Coming down the pier by the stairs we were all five together, and apart from battling with the waves, I had no feeling of apprehension or fear today. We swam against a very strong tide that seemed to keep us all rooted to the spot under the pier for what seemed ages. Swimming in treacle the others called it, it felt like ages but was presumably just seconds. My heart was beating fast and my legs were kicking the salt out of the sea, then with no warning, we all shot forward as the waves grabbed us and drove us to the shore. We landed in different places, having been separated by the waves, and we came in at completely different angles. But we did all come in, so I would suggest that it was a success! It definitely brightened my mood.

I told Natalie about the swim the other day and she went mental at me. I think it was the description of the walls of water and wondering if I had bitten off more than I could chew. Needless to say, she used the 'You've got kids,' line on me, and for once I had to agree. So I told her, quite genuinely actually, that I wouldn't go back, that I would hang up my goggles.

It seems I lied.

The thing is, and I think you understand this, I had to come again and I had to write it down. Lilly expects me to; she's insisting on it. What is that about? It's a dream, for Christ's sake, nothing else, just a bloody dream. But she won't leave me alone unless I write it down and she's making me do it here, in this shitty swimming arch and in this bloody diary.

It's been just a few months since I had that first dream about her and only two days since I was last in the sea. The last two nights I had the same dream I've had a few times now. Standing at the Old Steine, leaning against the railings in my jeans and T-shirt while the fishermen and the Sunday strollers looked right through me, leaving me there just waiting for her, hoping to catch her eye before she walks away. The frustration and rage in me was growing at not being able to chase after her. This morning I woke in a sweat again – the bed was literally wringing wet. Natalie was sure I must have had a fever in the night but I felt fine – at least in my body, if not my head. Even the kids kept their distance again this morning. I don't blame them; I woke up really anxious and must have looked dreadful.

The difference this morning, though, was that I had a burning desire to come to the arch and write this down. At one point, I felt I was even being pulled out of bed. I thought it was Alfie trying to pull me up to take him down to the kitchen for breakfast. Poor love, I shouted at him to leave me alone. I never shout at him, never. He literally jumped out of his skin and dived straight to Natalie. He'd actually been sitting at the bottom of the bed happily playing with some toys, doing nothing wrong at all. He burst into tears. Natalie looked at me like I'd gone nuts. But I'd thought he was pulling my hand and I just wanted to be left alone. It wasn't him, though; he wasn't anywhere near me. No one was. I didn't even apologise to him, or to Natalie for that matter, I just jumped up, threw on some clothes, and drove here, stopping on the way at the newsagents to buy a pack of pencils to write with.

God knows what Natalie will say when I get home, and Alfie! I want to go home and give him a huge hug and tell him how much I love him – it hurts so much to think I upset him like that.

It was Lilly, though, not me. I knew what she wanted me to do, I knew I had to come here.

Natalie wanted to put the diary down, but reading it made her feel like Adam was still with her. Even if it was the damaged Adam she was losing touch with, it was better than not having him at all. She turned to the next page and felt herself being drawn back into the life that was taken from her.

★★★

Daisy needed Jesse, and she needed him right away. "Where are you?"

The words came out of her mouth silently into the room, but in her mind she was screaming for him.

She was searching for him in every corner of her mind, but she couldn't reach out to him. She couldn't work out why he wasn't there; he was there every time before.

"Leave me alone, I don't want to come to you."

The room was silent as Daisy responded to a voice in her dream.

"How can I leave you alone when I am you?" the voice responded.

She knew she was still dreaming, but she was stuck there, unable to come back. She needed Jesse, he was always there at that moment in the dream, reaching out a hand, able to draw her back from the voice. In her dream, part of her knew that if she let herself go that she'd never come back, that she, Daisy, would never wake up. It took all her strength to fight it, every ounce, because the other part of her brain wanted to go. That part was telling her that Lilly loved her, that she and Lilly simply had to be together and that she must let go.

She needed Jesse to hold her back and to keep her safe from herself. She screamed again, "Jesse!"

This time his name split the silence of the room as she screamed out loudly.

★★★

"Mum, Mum!" Alfie ran screaming into Natalie's room.

Natalie looked at the clock and saw it was just past 4:30am. She had been glued to the diary for hours.

"Alfie, darling, what's wrong? Have you had a nightmare? Come here, sweetheart," she said, stretching out her arm while pulling back the duvet to give him space to crawl in beside her.

"Mum, it's Daisy. Quick," he said, grabbing her hand and pulling her from the bed.

Without asking what was wrong, she ran with him into the other room. "She's asleep, darling," Natalie whispered to her son. "Come on, get back into bed, you must have just had a bad dream."

"The lady's back. She's taking Daisy away!" Alfie screamed at Natalie. "Do something, Mum."

"Alfie, for goodness' sake, you'll wake her, just get back into bed."

"Mum!" he screamed again.

Natalie turned to Daisy to comfort her and say sorry for waking her up. But Daisy was not awake. She had not stirred at all, despite the noise.

"Mum, please." Alfie was desperate for Natalie's help and was pulling her towards the bed.

"Daisy. Daisy, wake up." Natalie's voice went from a whisper to a shout as she put her hands on her daughter's shoulder and gently shook her. She shook her harder, calling out her name as Alfie retreated back into the corner of the room, terrified.

"Daisy, for Christ's sake, wake up!" Natalie screamed at her again and again.

Daisy sat bolt upright, sending Natalie sprawling to the floor. Her eyes were wide open, taking in the scene around her.

Alfie ran forward, stepping over her and his mum as he grabbed his twin sister around the head and pulled her in close.

"Leave her alone. Leave my sister alone!" he screamed as he looked into the lifeless blue eyes that stared back at him.

Daisy took a deep breath, shut her eyes and fell back onto the pillow. When she finally opened her eyes again, they were the same green as they had always been, the same green as her brother's.

"Alfie, did you see her?" Daisy asked breathlessly.

"Yes."

"I told you she was real, didn't I? I told you."

Shaking and bewildered, Natalie took both her children in her arms and pulled them in close, not knowing what to say, or do.

"Can we come into your room for the rest of the night, Mum?" they asked in unison.

"Of course, darlings, of course."

Natalie pulled the twins in close, doing her best to shield them from the fear that had wrapped itself around them all, her hands shaking as she held them more tightly than she had ever done before. Once she had them tucked up in her bed, Natalie was about to climb in next to them when she spotted the diary on the floor. It had fallen off the bed when Alfie had come to get her. She considered it for a moment, wondering whether or not to pick it up.

It had fallen open near the end and, much as she tried not to, she couldn't help but read the words written by her husband.

I was there, last night, she took me back to her own time again and I saw it all. I could almost taste the energy in the room.

I wanted to help, to somehow stop her, but I couldn't. She had taken me there to see what happened; I couldn't do anything but stand and watch.

I was unable to do anything, not even warn them what she was about to do.

I wanted to scream at her to stop, but she wouldn't have heard me anyway. No one could hear me. I was only there to watch.

I ran out of the room after her and followed as she walked across the street towards the pier, even the wind unable to push her back. I ran into the road, but she was gone. The rain was thundering down, but not on me. I could sense it, hear it even, but I was not there, not really there. The door flew open behind me as someone in a cloak rushed out after her.

I need to stop her. I have to stop this happening, I have to do it to save our children, Natalie, forgive me, I have to do it, for Alfie and Daisy. I've no choice.

Natalie stared at the diary long after reading the last page.

"It was all in his mind, wasn't it? This wasn't real," she told herself.

But at the same time she knew what she had just seen when Daisy had opened her eyes – the eyes that had stared back at her were not her daughter's eyes.

She threw the diary across the room with all her strength. It hit the side of her dressing table and crashed to the floor, the papers fluttering to the carpet as the binding tore away.

Natalie climbed under the duvet and snuggled herself up as close as she could to the twins, amazed that they hadn't woken up with the crashing of the diary. She cocooned them as much as her stretched arms would allow her to and closed her eyes as the tears started to flow once again. She needed to sleep, needed to put everything aside and just sleep. She wouldn't let herself believe in ghosts. Lilly Baker wasn't real; she was just an illness her husband had. She was nothing but a dream that had driven her husband to his death. She was not, had never been, real.

CHAPTER TWENTY-THREE

Marlene

"It's four in the morning, my brain is not quite at *Jesse* speed yet, OK? Please sit yourself down, take a deep breath and start from the beginning; and slowly, if you don't mind."

Marlene had settled back into the cushion and brought the coffee cup up to her nose, letting the aroma stir her senses into life before taking a long slurp. Putting the cup on the armrest, she looked up at Jesse, giving him permission to start.

"I went to Adam's house..." he began. And then he stopped.

Marlene could almost see the adrenaline coursing around his body as he tried to find the right words to use.

She let the silence settle, taking another gulp of her coffee, then leaned forward.

"You met Adam's wife," Marlene prompted.

Jesse nodded and picked up his drink, turning his attention away from Marlene for a second.

Marlene could see something in his face, in the way he was avoiding eye contact with her.

"It seems she made an impression on you."

"You could say that."

"What happened?"

"It was pretty chaotic, actually. She thought her kids had gone missing, when I got there she was running all over the place. They were fine, though, just being kids, I guess. Her daughter – the one

186

I've been dreaming about – reacted as if it was the most normal thing in the world when she saw me standing there. She's a cool character, that kid."

"And what did Adam's wife say to that?"

"She was, well, suspicious, I guess. Anyway, we talked. Actually, I talked. It was all a bit crazy."

"Did she listen to you? Did you make her understand the danger she's in?"

"I tried. She settled the kids, got changed and then we talked. I think I might have been a bit direct."

"What did you say?"

"I told her I saw Adam. Recently."

"Oh, Jesse."

"What could I say? You weren't there, Marlene, it was, well, it was difficult."

"Exactly what happened? I want to know what you said."

"I told her about Adam and Lilly, and the diary. That and the fact that her ten-year-old daughter told her I was in her dreams and that she and I had a bond, I guess it sounded a bit… creepy. So the long and short of it is that I almost had my head taken off by a coffee cup and ended up running out of there."

"Oh, that's brilliant, really helpful! So now we're no further forward in getting the diary or finding out what Lilly has got against Adam and his kids and our best hope of finding out thinks you're some weird pervo. Brilliant work, Jesse."

"Well, it's not exactly quite as bad as that. Actually, I know a lot more than you think I do."

Marlene went quiet, as if she were listening to someone else for a moment.

"What is it?" Jesse asked her.

Her eyes were glazed over.

"Dad," Jesse whispered.

Marlene sank back even further into her chair, her head

shaking a little as her eyes focused once again.

"What happened last night, Jesse?"

"What was that I just saw?" he asked urgently.

"What did you see last night, Jesse? After you left Adam's house something happened, didn't it?"

"What did you just hear? Was it my dad?"

Marlene knew how desperate Jesse was to understand how she could hear his dad when he couldn't. It was like torture to him. Almost every day for nearly forty years he had seen or heard spirits, but never ones he wanted to hear; never his dad. And she knew that he blamed her for not helping him find a way to make contact; it was always there between them, threatening to one day tear their bond apart. But now wasn't the time to let that happen, she needed to know what he knew.

"What happened last night, Jesse? Tell me what you saw."

"After I left Natalie's, I needed some company. Female company."

Marlene said nothing and didn't react. She didn't care about that, she only cared about Adam Austin and Lilly Baker. She only cared about saving the life of two innocent children.

"After… well, after, you know, we fell asleep, and I dreamt. But it wasn't just a dream. I actually went back there; I was back with Lilly. I think I was John Austin."

Marlene didn't interrupt him as he told her what happened with Susie. She could see the turmoil in his face as he told her, but the only way for her to truly understand it was to help him call it back again, to feel it now.

As he leaned back into the chair, his eyes went cloudy.

"Breathe deeply, Jesse. In and out, slowly, in and out. That's it," she prompted him. "Tell me about John Austin, tell me what he felt."

"It was me first; I knew who I was. But then I was John Austin as well, we were both in my head. And I was with Lilly. She was waiting for me. She thought I was John, though, I didn't sense she knew it was me at the beginning, but then later, later…"

"Don't jump ahead, Jesse. Tell me as it happened. You were John Austin, and Lilly was with you…" she reminded him.

"She gave me the diary. I held it; it was as if the thing were alive, you know, like part of her, somehow. And we kissed. Actually, we… well, John, they made love. I couldn't tell if it was love, though. I mean, it was from her, I could see that in her eyes, she truly loved him. I've never had anyone look at me like that. It was hypnotic. She loved him so much."

Tears started to form in Jesse's eyes and he squeezed them shut as he carried on talking.

"But he didn't feel it back for her, not in his heart. I did feel love – strong love – but it wasn't for Lilly."

Jesse opened his eyes fully and stared ahead.

"Marlene, I looked deep into Lilly's eyes, deep into her soul and I knew she loved me, no John, I mean she loved John, and loved him so very much, but I could see she knew that he loved someone else. But she held on still, she wouldn't let him go."

"Then what?" she pressed again. "You said she tried to kill you?"

"I can't explain it exactly. I woke up to the sound of Susie screaming. She was on top of me. I was in her, sorry Marlene, I didn't mean…"

"I am an adult, Jesse," she said sarcastically. "Go on, she was on top of you and you were, you know, go on."

"She was strangling me. I could see she wanted to stop, but she couldn't. It wasn't her. Lilly had her, was her, and she was choking me. I managed to get her off me and… and came right here."

"Lilly possessed Susie and tried to kill you! Jesse, this is crazy, this shouldn't be happening. She shouldn't be able to do that."

"Well, she did!" he said aggressively. "I'm not making this shit up, you know."

"Sorry, I didn't mean that," she said, taking his hand to calm him down. "It's just, well, I've never heard, or read of anything like this before."

Jesse leaned forward and squeezed Marlene's hands urgently.

"I need to go back, Marlene. I have to go back there. I need you to send me back…"

Marlene pulled her hands away and stood up. "I won't do it, Jesse."

"Why not? We've done it before. You sent me back to the past before. That exercise we do – on the road – we've done it lots of times. What's the difference now? All I have to do is concentrate on the road and you send me back along it."

"I can't. Please, Jesse, you don't understand. I just can't." Marlene looked away, shaking her head.

Jesse jumped out of the chair and grabbed her by the shoulders, spinning her around until they were face to face, eye to eye.

"I don't understand? You're right, I don't understand!" he screamed in her face. "You want me to find out why Lilly took Adam and why she's after his children, but you won't help me do it. No, I don't understand! Tell me why. Make me understand."

"You're hurting me, Jesse," Marlene said, pulling herself back. Jesse's fingers were biting into her shoulders as his anger grew.

"Then help me, for Christ's sake. Help me save Natalie's children."

He pushed her backwards into her chair as he turned back to face the window. "And if you won't, then at least tell me why," he said, as he turned back around to face her once again.

"It's too dangerous. Your dad…" she hesitated a moment, scared to reveal the conversation between his dad and her. "It's just too dangerous."

"Tell me what he said." Jesse rounded on her again. "Tell me," he said with a slight menace in his voice.

"He's scared for you, Jesse. He can't help you there. Lilly is too strong for us – you and me. And your dad can't help; spirits can't help, they can only guide.

Jesse's anger turned to frustration.

He looked at her, his expression now full of sadness and pain. He took her arms again, this time gently, as if she were his grandmother.

"Take me to Dad then. Put me on the road and take me back to the crash. Show me what happened to my family. Help me understand, Marlene."

"Oh, Jesse."

"Please, Marlene, maybe if I understand what happened back then, maybe it'll help me understand the powers you think I've got now. Surely that's what you want, to help me understand?"

"You know it's just not possible for you to see your own family once they've passed over, that's just how it is."

"And you just told me it wasn't possible for Lilly to possess Susie and try to strangle me; but it happened, didn't it? How am I supposed to move forward, to learn how to control this gift, if I can't face my past? You say it's impossible, but you know I'm different. In your own words, 'You've never met anyone like me.' So, how the hell do you know what's possible or not? Is there some cosmic rule book in play that I don't know about?! Send me back, let me learn what happened to me. And then, maybe, I can learn to control my gift. Maybe that's the way I can save Daisy and Alfie, because at the moment we're saving no one; we're not even close to it."

She knew that this time she had no choice. She didn't think it was possible to do it, but she knew she had to try for him.

"I'll try. But I can't promise anything."

He hugged her close. "Thank you," he whispered.

She knew it would be hard, if not impossible to do. She knew, from her own experience and the experience of countless clients over the years, that trying to take someone back to someone they'd lost in a tragic accident was frowned upon by the spirit world. It could unleash feelings that could destroy you; it could bring back emotions that you were never meant to experience. But she also knew that if anyone could handle it then it had to be Jesse.

She led him back to the chair and sat him down before dimming the lights. She pulled the curtains closed and plugged her phone into the portable speaker she kept on the sideboard above the fireplace. She switched the phone to airplane mode so not to be disturbed and started the music playing a gentle, soulful jazz compilation, gently turning the sound down until it became just a background noise of saxophone, piano and trumpet.

"Close your eyes, Jesse. Settle back, find your comfortable position and take a deep, long breath." She said the words slowly and clearly, almost as if each word were a sentence in itself.

Marlene knew that Jesse understood the routine by heart, but still she gave him the instructions that she needed him to follow to the letter if this was going to have any chance of working.

He breathed deeply, taking in as much air as was comfortable.

"And slowly let it out," she continued at the same pace. "Release the air from your lungs, letting it out along with all the pain and worries that you are holding in. Blow them all out with the air until you have nothing left in you but air and light. Again, take another long, deep breath in and slowly let it out, again, in, out, in and out. Start to feel your toes, concentrate on them, move them, relax them, let them settle. As they settle and rest, move up to your ankles and do the same, relax them until they are steady. Up to your thighs, over your legs, slowly relaxing, still, heavy, calm."

With each word, Marlene slowed her voice further until she had taken Jesse up to his shoulders and head.

"S... l... o... w... l... y, c... a... l... m... l... y, y... o... u... r... h... e... a... d... i... s... h... e... a... v... y. Y... o... u... a... r... e... p... e... a... c... e... f... u... l."

Keeping her voice at the same low volume, Marlene moved

closer until she was seated only a couple of feet away from him and then she slowly returned to her normal speaking pace.

"You're on a road, Jesse. It goes just two ways, forwards and backwards, there are no other turnings and there is nothing but light on either side. You can choose to walk forwards and you can choose to walk backwards. Forwards takes you to places new, experiences yet to happen, people not yet met. Backwards takes you to stories gone, to people and places met, to both now and to before this life. I want you to turn around, Jesse, and take a single step back the way you came. Just one step. This first step is a symbol of where you wish to go, to a place once visited, to a time once lived. Now take another step. Think of the time, or the place, or the person you are searching for. Who are you looking for, Jesse? Step again, and again, pick up the pace to a walk and let yourself move towards your father and mother, and your sister. You are all together, Jesse. You are a family. Keep walking back. Keep walking. You are with your family, you are together. You are in a car. Where are you, Jesse? Can you see where you are?"

CHAPTER TWENTY-FOUR

Jesse

J esse was a child again, physically. He was in the back of a family car; his twin sister was sitting next to him giggling. She was singing the old French song, 'Frère Jacques' and Jesse found himself joining in with her when they got to the words *sonnez les matines*. As one, they changed the words to *funny semolina* and cracked up. His sister was laughing so hard that tears were gushing from her eyes and Jesse thumped his hands against the seat as he laughed with her.

The car was driving up a steep hill with a pine forest lining both sides. A group of cyclists came hurtling towards them down the hill, tears streaming down their faces as the speed of the air against their faces made their eyes weep. But they were not sad, far from it. They screamed in delight as they whooshed past. Jesse's father turned around to his children and smiled broadly at them.

"Turn around, Neil," Jesse's mother said to her husband. With a wink and a smile at the two giggling children, he turned back to the road. Next to his window, Jesse could see two more cyclists, this time going up the hill, pain etched onto their faces as the massive climb took its toll on their bodies; they dropped back as the car sped on. Jesse turned to watch them as they drove past.

The cyclists started to fade, and the warm summer sun, which a second ago filled the car, was replaced by a dark storm, the rain thundering in his ears. He wanted to scream. He tried to call his mum and dad, but their heads were no longer visible as the car started to sway in front of him. He turned his head to the left, but the seatbelt was holding him too tightly in place. He managed to focus on his sister next to him. She was still giggling, but Jesse could no longer hear her, she started to fade as the rain cascaded down his hair over his face.

In a burst of energy that left his body shaking as if it had been struck by a bolt of lightning, he found himself lying on the pavement on Brighton seafront. A storm was raging overhead and the rain was plummeting from the sky. He was lying in a puddle outside a hotel; he pulled himself up and saw a sign above him. 'Austin Hotel'.

He screamed into the night like a hurt animal, like a fearsome wolf. "Nooo! Nooo!"

He collapsed back onto his knees.

"Why now? Dad, why let me be pulled away now when I was so close to understanding? Why didn't you keep me with you?"

The tears of his anger mixed with the storm that raged above him quickly turned to tears of sadness.

"Why didn't I die with you? Why did you all have to leave me alone?"

He let himself wallow in the pain for what seemed like minutes but was only a few short seconds before his senses kicked in and he reacted to the feeling that something was burning into his head. Someone was watching him, willing him to look up and acknowledge them. He looked up from his place on the ground but saw nothing except the hotel looming above him.

Then, without warning, the main door was pushed open and from it came a face he had come to know all too well. Lilly Baker stood outside the hotel, the rain quickly soaking her, the clothes she wore sticking to her body like a second skin. He noticed for the first time a small bump forcing itself out from her dress; her strawberry blonde hair was plastered to her head, the ends being blown back by the wind. For the briefest of a millisecond, she caught Jesse's eye as he lay on the ground – a look that would have been imperceptible to anyone else, but to Jesse it was reaction enough and a challenge for him to follow. Lilly spun around and ran through the sheets of rain across the road, away from the hotel and all those inside, and away from Jesse. Frantically, he kept his eyes on her, but the rain had become so heavy that in no time Lilly was lost to him. He pulled himself up, the water pouring from his head and shoulders, but before he could move further, the door was thrown open once again and a cloaked figure ran past, following Lilly's hidden footsteps. Jesse was rooted to the spot, not sure if the door would open again to let another person loose on the storm, not sure if he should find a way to will himself back to Marlene and the time he was born into or take Lilly's unspoken invitation and follow her into the darkness. He sensed the eyes on him again. He knew it wasn't Lilly looking at him now. He spun around, but the eyes on him were not physical. Something was next to him, invisible, holding him back.

"Dad," he whispered into the howling wind. "I've got to follow her, Dad. I've got no choice."

The feeling left him and he was alone again. He was once again Jesse Daniels, alone and angry. "I've no choice!" he screamed into the rain as he sprinted after the cloaked figure.

The road was virtually deserted. The horses had been taken to safety by their owners and the usual crowds had dispersed to the relative dryness of the nooks and crannies from the many buildings that ran along the seafront. Through the rain, Jesse could see a large crowd gathered outside the entrance to the Chain Pier. They were dangerously close as the wind challenged the chains that the pier was named after. He ran to the crowd, his instincts drawing him forward. Jesse stood at the entrance to the pier, trying to get his bearings. The storm continued to scream overhead and the chains of the pier swung madly back and forth.

With the wind pummelling his face and the spray from the sea sticking his hair to his forehead, he lurched forward, past the blur of indistinct people and onto the pier. He found himself amidst a new crowd, this one in a panic and heading back along the pier to its entrance. The pier swung violently to the left, pushing Jesse into the path of a man dragging his children and wife to safety. More people came, couples dragging each other as they were thrown left and right, pier staff ushering people to the safety of the promenade and men desperate to save their friends and families from the storm that had caught them all unawares. As he moved against the tide of people, crashing through to find a clearing, he spotted Lilly. He had to get to her, she was pulling him closer, sharing with him the story that he desperately needed to understand. What he did now was everything – there was no more 2021, there was only now. The thought jarred him like a lightning bolt, just as a thundering wave hit the pier, throwing the platform under him high into the air, knocking him off balance and sending him falling to the floor. Twisting onto his side, he saw the cloaked figure up ahead moving closer to Lilly. It was so quick and so sudden he couldn't make out the shape, he had no way of knowing if it was a man or a woman, a friend or a foe to Lilly.

Jesse pulled himself up and rushed forward, managing to hold onto the side rail as it leapt once more into the air. Lilly was suddenly standing in front of him, almost stationary, while the floor she was standing on was violently thrown from side to side. She held his eyes, like she had that very first time he had seen her under the pier, willing him to join her. He couldn't stop himself; each step took him not only towards her but also back into the mind of John Austin. It took all his willpower, every bit of strength he had to stop the past taking control of his mind. He was *not* John Austin. And he was not Adam Austin.

"I am Jesse Daniels!" he screamed through the wind to himself, as he forced his way forwards against it.

The wind continued to build and the waves threw themselves into the pier from every angle, shaking it to its core. It made the short walk almost impossible, but Jesse kept going. He had no fear for his own life; the only thought in his mind was making it to Lilly, to end her hold over the Austin family, to save Natalie's children. He was so close now; she was just feet away. He watched as the cloaked figure reached her first.

John Austin screamed in his head, making Jesse stagger with its ferocity. Closing his eyes tightly and shaking his head, Jesse screamed: "Noooo, you will not get in my head, I will not let you control me."

He opened his eyes again – his eyes, not John Austin's eyes – and his mind.

Within just a few feet of him, the first chain came loose. He heard it milliseconds before he felt it, a booming sound like a whip being used against an animal as it sprung at the circus master, splitting the air into small pieces as it cut like a knife through butter. Jesse's feet were taken from under him, leaving him suspended in mid-air as the platform gave way and he fell downwards, coming to a jolting stop as the other chains took up the weight, the loose chain cutting through the air and tearing through the section of floor just inches from where he had been standing. He crashed back onto the floor as the pier was being ripped apart under him. Scrambling up, he tried to find a handhold that would stop him sliding down the half-broken floor and falling into the murderous sea below. His fingers dug into the broken floorboard, gripping them with all his strength. The pain and stress in his wrists and arms was only marginally less excruciating than the pain of the splinters of wood as they pierced his knuckles. He turned his head towards the place he had last seen Lilly and the cloaked figure.

The two bodies in front of him were spun around. Lilly fell to the edge of the pier and Jesse saw the cloaked figure pull a metal object from under the cloak and swing it at Lilly's head, catching her with a glancing blow and sending her crashing to the ground; the wind and the howling rain suddenly dragged them both further into the centre of the pier.

Willing the strength back into his body, Jesse pulled himself back up and launched himself towards them both. He literally flew through the air, the floor of the pier springing up to give him the extra height he needed, sending him flying into the bodies of Lilly and her assailant, as the wind pulled and pushed him with equal intensity. He reached out to a small hand and stretched himself beyond his reach, grabbing two hands, from two different bodies. Desperation flooded over him as they each clung to him for dear life. His feet were pressed against the side of the pier as he tried to pull them both up and away from the maelstrom below and his mind screamed to save the lives of people already long dead.

He squeezed the two hands as tightly as he could, the blood running down his wrist from the splinters as they dug deeper into his flesh and ran over their hands, joining them all together, his blood and their blood. His grip was slipping. He was holding them both, one in each hand, but they were slipping down, further and further to the sea.

"Pull!" he cried above the sound of the wind. "Pull yourselves up. I can hold you both, I can hold you... climb!"

The sound of the wind stopped. There was utter silence. The pier moved violently, but Jesse was still, no more pain in his hands, no straining of muscles.

"Save me, help me, Jesse," he heard in his head. It was Lilly. Absolute calmness, her voice no louder than a whisper. "Save me, Jesse."

Another wave hit the side of the pier. Jesse was thrown back, dangerously close to the gaping hole in the floor. A body crashed into him, thrown back onto the pier like a rag doll by the force of the wave. Just one body. Covered in a cloak and hood. It moved quickly; it was alive. It stood and staggered swiftly away from him, away from the decimated pier and back to the entrance.

The storm, having thrown its last powerful punch, ended as quickly as it had begun. The blue sky broke through a cloud, throwing some light onto the pier.

"Lilly!" Jesse screamed. "Lilly…"

He pulled himself up and rushed to the hole that had been torn into the pier floor and stared down into the abyss. The waves were huge mountains of water rolling under the pier and heading to the shore.

The pier was once again filling with people, all running towards him, some shouting words of comfort, others running to the side, eyes scanning the water, looking for a trace of life.

Lilly was gone.

"Lilly," he said through the noise of the crowd.

"She's there, I can see her!" a voice shouted.

Jesse ran to the side, the crowd seeing him as if he should be there, not as an interloper from the future. Some tried to grab him to stop him falling over while others reached out to prevent him from doing what he knew he had no choice but to do.

Without any thought for where or who he was, he launched himself from the side of the pier and into the depths of the sea. He surfaced into a huge wave that spun him over and forced water down his throat, causing him to gag as he rose again, just in time for another wave to crash into him and force him under again. Spitting the water from his mouth, he grabbed a deep breath on his next surface and spun around and around, looking over the water, scanning the waves around the pier, but she was nowhere. He dived under just as another wave came crashing over him and swam down into the depths of the sea, but it was too dark; he couldn't see anything. His lungs were screaming for air and his eyes burnt with the sea salt that washed through them. He had to surface; he needed air. He kicked hard but he didn't move. He kicked again, but he was caught. Something, or someone, had his leg, it was pulling him down. His life flashed before him. He was back in the car with his twin sister giggling next to him. His mum and dad were in the front, turning and smiling at him. He smiled back. He was safe again, they had come back for him; it was time to join them at last, to be a family again.

CHAPTER TWENTY-FIVE

Marlene

Marlene was doing everything she could but Jesse wasn't responding. One minute she was guiding him down the road back to a time that he had so desperately wanted to visit, and the next his face had turned blue and his breathing had gone from long, deliberate breaths to nothing, not a breath. His chest was no longer moving. He started to choke. He was drowning right in front of her. It made no sense; he was lying back in the armchair in her lounge in Hurstpierpoint, it was four-thirty in the morning and he was drowning. She took him by the shoulders and started shaking him as hard as she could, screaming his name, the sound of a lone saxophone circling the room from her speaker. She pulled and pushed at him but there was no response. He was dying in front of her and she couldn't do anything about it. It was almost two minutes since she had last seen him draw a breath and if it went on any longer she knew that she would never be able to get him back; even seconds now could mean the difference between life and death, or for Jesse even worse, an oxygen-starved brain that could no longer function like a human needed it to.

"Think, Marlene," she said to herself as she stood up and stared at her friend. "What would Marlene the teacher do, not Marlene the friend? The teacher would go in there and pull him out," she heard herself say. Against all logic and fighting a natural instinct to shake and pound him further, she sat back down in her chair. She closed her eyes, shut out the noise in the room and took a deep, deep breath and slowly exhaled. She breathed deeper than she had ever breathed in her life. She took air and light into her body and exhaled away all the pain and worries that life was throwing at her. She breathed in, exhaled again and again until her body relaxed. She put herself on the road that she had set so many students on over the years. In her mind, she walked to the side road. Jesse was somewhere else, but he was also here, right here and right now, and he needed her to bring him back onto the road. She stepped off the road into nothingness.

★★★

His sister's face started to fade. His parents were drifting, leaving him again.

"Don't go," he pleaded. "Not again. Don't leave me again."

His brain screamed with fear at the same time as his lungs struggled for one last breath. He felt himself start to rise. The hands trying to pull him down were still there, but there was something else now, something above him pulling him up. He didn't know which one to fight for. He wanted his family and he knew that going down further would take him there, take him back to them. But there was another voice. A voice calling him – a voice he knew and loved. It was calling him and pulling him upwards. It was a voice he trusted. A voice that cared, that was maybe not blood, but was family, nonetheless. He found himself reacting to it, kicking against the hands below with every ounce of strength he had left.

He burst back into the light. She was there with him, back in the lounge. The waves crashing around him were gone and there was now nothing but the sounds of Marlene's favourite jazz quartet. The raging storm that had held him in its grip was gone, replaced by a sunrise, throwing the first ray of morning over him through the lounge window.

Jesse was in his chair, his eyes open and his chest heaving as he drew air back down into his lungs, filling them once again with life. He watched as Marlene came to, opened her eyes and burst into tears as she stared into Jesse's face as his colour slowly returned.

"I thought I'd lost you," she said between sobs.

"You brought me back? It was you I heard," he said.

She was the family he'd never had; he knew that now. She had risked her own life by falling into his past to get him and she had done it out of love for a child, out of the love she had in her heart for him.

"I saw them," he said.

He could see from her reaction that she did not quite understand who he meant by 'them'. She had tried to send him back to his family, but he knew that she did not believe it was possible. He understood that she had only done it to try to calm him down and take him into a meditative state. But he had gone somewhere, he had gone somewhere and almost not come back.

"Who did you see?" she asked nervously.

"My family. My dad, my mum, my sister."

"It's not possible," Marlene whispered.

"You sent me back to my parents."

"It can't have been them," she said. "It's not possible. Everyone knows it's not possible. Every book ever written about spirits, every book for hundreds, thousands of years, every person who understands, all of us, we all know it's not possible to visit the time that has shaped your life in the way your family's death shaped yours. It's too challenging for the soul, it can't take that level of pain, or love, it's too much – it would kill you."

"I was there," he said with complete conviction. "I was in the car with them. On a steep hill. It was the Ventoux. I know it was.

There were cyclists, and there were trees around us. I was there, we were driving up Le Mont Ventoux in Provence."

"It's just not possible," she whispered again.

"You always said I was different, stronger."

"I know; you are, but…"

"I was there, Marlene. You sent me back," he repeated. "You need to believe me."

Marlene leaned back in her chair. "My God, Jesse, it's… it's…"

"I know," he said. "You showed me a story about the ghost hunter, Marlene. You said she had been the only one. Well, maybe she wasn't. Maybe, you're right. Maybe, I really am one too. I need to go back again, I have to know what happened to us, what caused the crash. Why I didn't die with them; I should have but something stopped me."

"But you nearly died just now, Jesse. The experience nearly did kill you right in front of me. I can't risk it again, what if this time I am not able to find you or pull you out? What if you're there and I can't find your father again? No, it's too much of a risk, I won't do it."

"You don't understand…"

"I do understand, perfectly," she said fiercely. "I watched you stop breathing. You were drowning, sitting in that chair. I saw it. I pulled you back."

"It wasn't seeing my family that was killing me, Marlene. It was Lilly. She pulled me back again."

"What?"

"It was Lilly, she pulled me away from my parents. I was with them and she pulled me out and took me back to her. I was on the pier with her."

Jesse got up and walked into the kitchen to get her a glass of water. "Sip this," he said when he came back a few seconds later.

She drank the water then took a deep breath before standing up and walking over to the fireplace.

"We need to record all this; I can't miss anything."

She picked up her mobile phone and set its record function to on.

Jesse told her everything. He told her about the car journey first so she could understand what he had felt sitting next to his twin sister and seeing his parents. And then he told her about Lilly, how she pulled him away, and he told her about the cloaked figure on the pier.

"So, she was murdered, then. This cloaked figure pushed her and she fell off the pier and drowned. Did you not see his face? Do you think it was John Austin who killed her?"

"I don't know; it could have been, I guess."

"But you saw a man in a cloak chase her across the road?"

"I never said that. I said I saw a cloaked figure, but I don't know if it was John Austin. I don't know. I need to go back, Marlene. You need to send me back so we can see who it was and find out why."

"No way, Jesse. No way. It's out of the question. You almost died."

"But I didn't, did I? I could have saved her. I could have pulled Lilly out of the sea and saved her and then who knows, maybe all this would never need to happen."

"You couldn't save her, it's already happened, you can't change that, and it doesn't sound like that's why she took you there," Marlene said, shaking her head. "Have you not listened to anything I've ever told you? She died, Jesse, someone murdered her. But you couldn't have saved her, you can't change what's happened. She wants to finish her revenge and destroy any future for the Austin family; just like she took Adam Austin's life, she needs to now take his children, and if we're in the way then she'll kill us as well."

"That's why you need to send me back, let me do something to stop this."

"I can't. Next time she could kill us both, it's too dangerous.

We need to know who killed her, and why, and then we can use that to work out how to stop her."

"So how do we do that if I don't go back?"

"We need that diary he left. Adam saw something, maybe Lilly showed him the truth and he recorded it in the diary. If he saw something, then maybe he wrote it down. We need to get that diary from Natalie."

★★★

Daisy shook Alfie awake, making sure she kept one hand over his mouth so as not to disturb Natalie who was fast asleep next to them.

"What is it?" he whispered to her, having forced her hand away and stifled a yawn.

"She wants to see us," she replied in a dreamy voice. "Come with me, Alfie," she said, firmly taking his hand.

Careful not to wake Natalie, she led him down the hall to their own room. She walked to the bedroom window that faced their back garden patio and pulled back the blinds. Below them, Lilly gazed up and smiled. Daisy smiled back as her brother's eyes slowly closed, sending him back into a peaceful sleep.

"Come with me, Alfie," Daisy whispered to her brother. "She wants us to go now."

Without a break in their steps, Daisy led Alfie, whose eyes were still closed, down the stairs and of out the front door, which she shut carefully behind them so as not to cause any disturbance in the house. The front gate opened and Daisy and Alfie followed Lilly out of the driveway onto the road, Lilly's perfume leading them on as if she were the pied piper leading her children into a nightmare.

CHAPTER TWENTY-SIX

Natalie

atalie woke with a start. She lay there for a minute, trying to remember everything that had happened last night. Trying to separate in her mind the fact from fiction; the things she remembered happening between her and Adam and the things he claimed to have seen and done in another place or another time. She thought back to last night and what had happened to Daisy, and what she saw in Daisy's eyes. Her head ached from all the thinking and all the tears she had shed. She glanced down and saw the diary, still lying where she had thrown it the night before. There were some loose papers scattered next to it, which must have fallen out when she'd thrown it across the room and broken the binding.

The sun was only just rising and starting to leak through her bedroom blinds. She lay there for another moment, enjoying the silence. Then it struck her that the twins were not there. She sat bolt upright. They had slept with her last night, after Daisy's nightmare. She had brought them back to her room. They must have crept out in the night and gone back to their own room. They would be curled up together on Alfie's bed like they always were, she decided. She'd let them sleep some more. They would be shattered after last night and if she woke them up now they'd be a nightmare all day. She'd give them another half an hour and then go and check on them.

208

She climbed quietly out of bed, gathered up the diary and the loose pages, turning them over in her hands. She reopened the diary and for the first time saw a place at the back where pencils or papers could be kept. The papers must have been in there all along. She put the diary back down and looked closely at the three loose pages. The first one was a sketch of a rowing boat and a girl. She smiled to herself. Adam always fancied himself as an artist, but really, he was less than average at best. She would always find little drawings on newspapers or in the back of books, even over the children's homework. He sometimes didn't even realise he was doing it. She lifted the page to her nose and breathed in the carbon from the pencil. It was the closest she could get to him now, she thought sadly, as she realised all that was left of her husband were a few old sketches of little importance. She carefully put the page in the drawer next to her bed; something to show the children later, she thought, and she smiled at the thought of their reaction.

She picked up the second page. It looked like a family tree. It was written in his handwriting, but it was just first names and years. She didn't recognise any of them apart from the final four; Adam's late dad, Adam himself and the twins. She put the page back in the fold in the diary and picked up the last page. Adams words seemed to have been written in a hurry as they were all smudged and the lines ran into themselves. He must have written it when he didn't have the diary with him and then stuffed it in the back.

DIARY

> *I'm scared.*
>
> *Lilly is pregnant. And so is Mary. John is the father to both of them. Last night I dreamt I was back in the Austin Hotel. It wasn't me, though. I was John Austin again, I was my own great-grandfather; it's too hard to explain, it's almost impossible to write.*
>
> *I have to go back; I have to physically go back again. I have to go back to when it happened. I need to stop it; I have to do it to*

WHAT THE TIDE BRINGS BACK

save our children. If I stop it happening back then, maybe it'll stop her doing this now.

Natalie, forgive me, I have to do it. I've no choice.

The words ended. That was all he had written. It was like the rantings of a madman, but he had believed it all, Natalie knew he had believed everything he had written, even that he could go back in time and stop it all from happening – whatever *it* was.

Natalie dropped the paper on her bed as the tears took over once again. Adam had gone into the sea the same morning that he'd written that note and now she knew that he had meant to go in, but she also knew that he hadn't wanted to. It was never suicide. He hadn't wanted to die. The police had it all wrong.

He had gone into the sea to save his children.

She turned to the clock again; it was past 7am now and the house was still quiet.

"Guys," she called out, half yawning.

The silence that came back to her was deafening.

"Guys?" she called again, this time a note of urgency in her voice. "Alfie – Daisy. Come on, it's getting late."

A feeling of dread worked its way into her stomach. Throwing the covers aside, she rushed next door into Alfie's room. The blinds were wide open and the nightlight was still on from last night when she had come in, but the room was silent.

The bottom bunk, Alfie's bed, was empty. Slowly, she stood on his mattress and hauled herself up to Daisy. Hesitantly, she peered over the top. Her bed was empty as well. It had been well slept in, the duvet bunched up at the end and Bruno, her faithful toy dog, was lying alone on the mattress.

The panic clawed at her throat.

"Daisy!" she screamed. "Don't you dare mess me about! Come out now – you too, Alfie."

She jumped down from the bed and ran out of the room,

crashing into the side of the door as she went. She barged through the open door into the spare room. It was as empty as it always was.

She instinctively knew this was not like the other time when the twins had hidden themselves away in the gym. The butterflies in her stomach told her that they were not in the house. Fear rooted her to the spot, all powers of speech temporarily unplugged, her senses started shutting down. Her legs buckled and she could feel them wobble. She had to fight it off, she couldn't lose control, not now.

She found her way back into her room and grabbed the phone. She dialled 999; the call was answered almost immediately.

"Which service?" came the reply.

"Police, please, sorry, the police please."

"Certainly, madam. Can I ask you what the emergency is?"

"My children are missing; I've lost my children..." the enormity of it all overcame her. She collapsed onto the floor, the phone sliding away from her as it hit the carpeted floor. Tears streamed down her face, her body wracked with sobs.

"Madam, are you there? Madam, can you hear me?" the operator repeated. Natalie couldn't speak. She lay on the floor, helpless, curled into a ball sobbing.

Downstairs the doorbell rang.

Believing it was the children, that somehow they had got locked outside, she pulled herself up and ran down the stairs, three at a time, and hit the gate button in case they were outside in the street.

She pulled the front door open, expecting the children to fall into her arms, laughing at their stupid joke; she would forgive them anything now, even this.

"Natalie, what's wrong?" asked Jesse as he saw Natalie standing there, the fear and worry of a desperate mother etched onto her face. "What's happened?" Jesse asked again as he and Marlene walked into the house. Marlene instinctively took control, led Natalie into the hallway and sat next to her on the blue velvet chaise longue that formed the centrepiece of the large open space.

Natalie suddenly sprang into action again and went to jump up, remembering the police she had left on the phone.

"Whoa, whoa," Jesse said, standing in front of her. "Slow down. What's happened?"

"The children," Natalie gasped. "They're not in their bed."

"OK, have you looked around the house? The treehouse again? Or the gym?" Jesse said.

"It's seven in the fucking morning!" she screamed at him, as she pushed past and ran back up the stairs.

"Natalie, I'll search the garden and the downstairs, Marlene will help you upstairs," Jesse called to Natalie as he ran through the hallway heading into the lounge.

Marlene ran up the stairs and found Natalie holding the phone to her ear. "Yes, that's right, my children. I know full well what time it is and yes I've looked around the house. What? No, not in my garden. No, not in the kitchen, either. I thought… what? OK, I'll go look. OK, OK, I'll call you right back."

She slammed the phone down frustrated and turned to Marlene.

"I tell them my children are missing and they tell me to look in the bloody garden."

"Well, maybe we should," Marlene said gently.

"Who the hell are you?" Natalie said, suddenly realising there was a stranger in her room with her. "And where's Jesse?"

"Sit down, Natalie."

"What!"

"Please sit down. We can help you, but I need you to focus." Marlene said the words slowly and deliberately.

Her soothing tone allowed Natalie to calm herself a little and take stock of the moment. She sat down on the bed.

ROB STARR

"I'm Marlene, a friend of Jesse's."

"The medium?"

"I consider myself his teacher. But, yes, I guess you can call me that."

"You know about Adam, then? About this Lilly he was obsessed with?"

"Lilly is real, Natalie. At least her spirit is. And yes, I know a lot about her. But I need to know more. If Lilly has taken them…" Marlene didn't want to finish the sentence. "Let us help find your children. I need you to trust us, Natalie. Let us help you, please. The police can't help, not with this. And they won't believe it. They'll have you running all over town hunting down God knows who, and we don't have time for that. Let Jesse and me help you find them. You need to help us understand what Adam knew. We *can* save your children; I promise you, we can."

Natalie was torn. One part of her, the sane, sensible part, wanted to call the police back. But what had the police done for her when Adam went missing? They called it suicide and filed it away. They didn't even try to find out the truth, and then they left her alone with her children and with her pain. And now she'd read the diary and she knew about Lilly. Adam had believed it all, every word. And she had trusted Adam all her life. Over the fifteen years they had been married, he had been everything to her; he had been her true love. She had trusted him without question; she wanted to trust him now as well, however crazy it sounded.

Jesse came into the bedroom breathless.

"Nothing," he said. "I've checked everywhere. They're not here."

"Natalie, please, tell us everything you know," Marlene asked, the urgency in her voice coming through in its clipped tones.

Natalie looked from one to the other and then grabbed the phone back to call the police again; to do something logical, practical even.

Jesse snatched the phone off her.

"You need to trust us, Natalie. Look at how Daisy reacted when she saw me; she knew me and trusted me; and we'd never even met before. Something's happening here that none of us can really explain, but it goes beyond real logic. I can see it in your face, you know you should believe us, just as Adam would want you to. Do it now, Natalie, take this leap of faith and let us help you."

CHAPTER TWENTY-SEVEN

Jesse

Natalie told them what she could remember from the diary. This time there were no tears, just pure focus on finding her children, even if it meant trusting two strangers and a crazy story. Jesse didn't question any of it, he had seen, experienced even, much of it himself.

"Can I see the diary?" Jesse asked.

"I've told you everything I read, there's nothing in there that can help us."

"It's not what's in there that Jesse needs to see, Natalie," Marlene said, leaning over and picking up the diary. "May I?" she asked. Natalie nodded. Marlene handed it to him. He touched it reverently. He ran his fingers over its old leather skin and then closed his hands around it. He closed his eyes and shut down the left side of his brain, and engaged the right side, the side that held his gift, his curse.

"What's he doing?" Natalie asked.

"Shh," Marlene whispered, taking Natalie's hand in hers. "Let him sense her, she's in there somewhere, in the diary. He can feel her."

Jesse opened his eyes almost instantly.

"They're with Lilly. I... sorry, it's impossible; I can't explain it in words that I think you'd understand."

"Well, you'd better fucking try!" Natalie shouted at him.

"What is this bullshit?" she said, turning to Marlene. "Someone's got my children and he can't explain it in words I'll understand? I'm calling the police."

She reached for the phone as Marlene put her own hand on Natalie's. "Give him a chance, Natalie, please. Jesse, try, tell her what you know," Marlene instructed him.

"Look, all I can tell you is that I know what I know, OK. Lilly somehow has the children. It's kind of like they are still in a dream and they can't wake up. Not a bad dream, it's not a nightmare, they're still together, it's just like a dream that they're both part of. That's all they'll remember when they wake up. Lilly can't harm them yet, that I know for sure, otherwise, well, I could sense an urgency in her, that she would have done something by now. I think she needs to be at a certain place before she can do anything; until then, she's still just a dream to them as well. Nothing more than a vision. I need to go," he said, turning quickly for the bedroom door.

"Where to?" Marlene asked.

"The Queens Hotel."

"Are the children there?" Natalie asked, desperation creeping into her voice.

"I don't think so; I couldn't see them. But I know it started there."

"What started there, Jesse?" Marlene asked.

"Everything did," he said, looking up again, catching the eyes of both Natalie and Marlene. "All of it did."

Without another word, Jesse turned, the diary still clutched in his hands, and stalked out of the bedroom, down the stairs and out of the front door.

★★★

"What the hell did that mean? How's that going to help find my children?"

Natalie wanted to believe that Marlene and Jesse could help, but the bigger part of her wanted to call the police and start getting practical now.

"I don't know what it means; I doubt Jesse does either. But it seems to me that the key to getting your children back is to find out where Lilly has to go, and I think I might know someone who can help us."

"I need to call the police," Natalie said again.

"We will call them; I promise we will. But the children aren't in any danger yet; I believe Jesse on that, and I can see in your eyes that you do as well. The police will only get in the way at the moment, Natalie." Marlene took Natalie's hand in her own and looked deep into her eyes. "Please trust me, Natalie. We'll find your children, I promise. You've read Adam's diary; you've listened to his story. And you've seen Lilly, I know you have. Even if not in the body, you've tasted her perfume, haven't you? You know she's real. I know deep down in your heart you believe me, that's why you're torn between what your head tells you to do and what your instincts are telling you to do. Trust your instincts, Natalie, please. They are far more powerful than you could ever imagine."

Natalie had to make a decision, she knew time was now against them, she had to choose what and who to believe.

It was the single hardest decision she would ever have to make. In a split second, she tried to picture herself in front of the police spending time trying to explain everything to them, knowing that whatever she said to them it would ultimately have to include ghosts and suspicions. She knew there was no way that conversation would go well. And she remembered clearly how abandoned she'd felt after they had told her Adam had committed suicide. The alternative was to put her faith in these relative strangers; two people who seemed to know more about her life and her family than they ever should.

"Natalie, time is running out; you need to trust us," Marlene said.

"I'm only doing this because Daisy trusts him," Natalie replied, her decision finally made.

She took the loose papers from her drawer, the ones that had fallen from the diary, and handed them to Marlene.

"I only found these this morning," she said. "This page must mean something."

She moved one particular page to the top. It was the handwritten family tree written by Adam.

She left Marlene to look at the papers while she threw on some clothes.

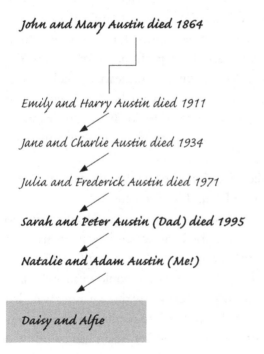

John and Mary Austin died 1864

Emily and Harry Austin died 1911

Jane and Charlie Austin died 1934

Julia and Frederick Austin died 1971

Sarah and Peter Austin (Dad) died 1995

Natalie and Adam Austin (Me!)

Daisy and Alfie

On the reverse of the paper were details of each person on the list, focusing on the men who had all died young. Marlene read the paper word for word and was staggered at all the deaths that had defined the history of the Austin family.

Dressed and with her hair tied hastily into a bun, Natalie felt determined; she was not going to give up so easily. Adam had done all he could to save their children, even giving up his life, and so she would do the same if needs be, even if it meant trusting these strangers and going up against something that she barely understood.

"The answer is in here, Natalie," Marlene said, showing her the family tree. "Something has been killing the Austin men down the years and the list is almost complete."

"You don't mean something, do you, you mean someone?" Natalie said.

Marlene nodded. "This paper is the key, I'm sure of it. We need to find out what happened to them all; and where."

"But how can that help? They are all long dead; even Adam," she said firmly. "Are you telling me that you think they died the same way? Surely someone would have put that together before now?"

"Maybe, maybe not. But if there is a pattern here then it could lead us to your children. It's got to be worth trying? Please, Natalie, trust me; just give me an hour, and if I can't show you anything, then you can call the police. Just an hour?"

Natalie was so torn. Every logical sense told her to call the police back; her children were missing and every second counted, let alone an hour. But the diary; Adam's words. If Lilly was real, if by some mad stretch of the imagination Lilly was real and had taken her children, then it was Jesse she needed now and not the police.

"An hour," she said reluctantly. "Just an hour. And God forbid you're wrong and something happens to them…" she trailed off.

"An hour," Marlene repeated.

Without another word, they left the house. Jesse had taken Marlene's car, so it meant they had to go in Natalie's.

"Maybe I should drive," Marlene said, holding out her hand for the keys.

"They are my children. Wherever we have to go, I'll be taking us, OK. And exactly where is it we are going?"

"A friend of mine, she lives in the North Laines. She's a genealogist, world renowned as it happens."

"How's she meant to help us?" Natalie said with frustration, already questioning herself as to why she chose to trust Marlene and Jesse rather than the police.

"We need to find out where and how the Austin men died, and if anyone knows how to find that out, it's Sofia. You need to trust me, Natalie, please."

"Get in," Natalie said, unlocking the door and taking her place behind the wheel.

Twenty minutes later, they pulled up outside the home office of Sofia Montez. The house was a small mid-terrace property in Gardner Street in the North Laines. It was squeezed in between two coffee shops, one a small independent shop like so many that had sprung up all over the city and the other a large coffee chain franchise that was opening up in equally large numbers every time an independent opened, supposedly to try to force them out of business. Both seemed to be doing a roaring trade this morning, defying the battle lines that had been drawn. Sofia's house, nestled in between, still had the frontage of an old shop at ground level. In the window, hidden behind old net curtains, were hundreds, if not thousands, of pieces of old cork scattered along the deep window ledge and surrounding a huge sailing ship, also built entirely out of cork, that had once been the centrepiece of the cork shop that had stood there for 125 years before it closed down fifty years before. The property was still owned by the last surviving family member, Sofia Montez. Rather than convert the shop into yet another eating or drinking establishment, Sofia had moved from her small flat in the city centre into the maisonette upstairs and then converted the shop below into an office, from where she could follow her passion for genealogy and export her findings around the world. She was one of the world's foremost experts in the lives and deaths of others, and her skills were in demand from people looking for either the ideal birthday gift for their grandmother's eightieth birthday or by governments looking to establish the rights and ownership of pieces of land that had been in dispute for centuries.

Natalie found a parking space almost right outside and turned off the engine, before taking a huge breath, wondering where this was now going to take them.

"She's fantastic, really," Marlene said as they approached the front door.

"But?"

"Let's just say that she has more energy than most people half her age. That alone is fine, if not a little exhausting, but she also likes to share a lot of information. I think her brain works two steps ahead of everyone else's and, coupled with that, she has an intellect far beyond most people. You shouldn't be afraid to move her on if she starts getting into all the finer detail, otherwise we could be here for hours."

Natalie looked at her watch and reminded Marlene that they didn't have hours; in fact, the clock was ticking fast on the hour she'd already agreed to. Just as they were about to ring the bell, Sofia emerged from the Small Batch coffee shop next door holding a steaming takeaway of her favourite soya latte.

"Marlene!" she screeched in her standard high octave English, which was layered under a strong Spanish lilt.

Despite being well into her eighty-fifth year, Sofia Montez had an energy for life that had made her a local legend.

"You wanna coffee, you and your friend?" she asked, giving Natalie a one-armed hug so as not to spill her own coffee. "Come, this way," she said, leading them from Small Batch to Starbucks on the other side. "I like to support both my neighbours, of course, all coffee is good, room for everyone." She laughed out loud. "Come, come, latte for you both, yes?"

"We've not much time," Marlene said to her friend.

"Never have, my darling, do you? Make time for coffee, though, always time for good coffee while we talk. Come, come; we get takeaways for you both, then you come to my house." Sofia took Natalie's hand in hers. "Whatever it is, my darling, Sofia will help. Come, come; coffee first."

Minutes later, with cups of coffee in hand, the three of them settled into Sofia's office next door. The walls were covered with her own family photos, old and new.

She watched as Natalie looked over them.

"My family is beautiful, yes? I love putting the old and the new together. See, even though centuries separate us, we still have the same round faces, same colouring and same beautiful figures. Ah, I miss my Harry, such a funny man, always making me laugh, ha." Despite her age, Sofia still had the slim figure of a lady a quarter of her age. "See my children there, beautiful, yes? And so many grandchildren, and great-grandchildren. I am truly blessed. I'm too young to have so many, you're thinking, ha. And you, you have children, yes?"

"Yes," Natalie said with a wobble in her voice.

"I talk too much, much too much. I have said something sad, yes? Come, come, to my desk, what can we do for you, come, come," she said, pushing Natalie into the centre of the room to sit at a large round wooden dining table that was covered with books and papers, and, in the centre, proudly commanding, was the most up-to-date computer and printer on the market. Marlene sat down on the other side of Sofia. She handed her the family tree that had fallen from the diary.

"Ah, I see," Sofia said, focusing her eyes on the paper and touching the small keyboard, springing the screen into life. Her fingers flew deftly across the small keyboard like those of an eighteen-year-old who had been born into the high-tech world of computers.

Natalie marvelled at the speed at which Sofia moved the history on the screen as Marlene took up the mantle of orator by reading from Adam's family tree.

"Lilly Baker, died around 1864, lived in Brighton, London born we think, orphaned as a baby, probably around the early 1840s, brought up on Rose Street in the St Anne's orphanage, prime suspect in the brutal murder of one of the fathers, a Father Stevens if I remember correctly. Worked in the Austin Hotel for John and Mary Austin in the mid-1800s. Adam Austin, drowned 2012, suspected suicide off Brighton Beach near the Palace Pier. John Austin was his grandfather, great-great, I think? We believe he was murdered as well but it's undocumented. Harry Austin, John and Mary's son. He died young, details unknown. Harry left a widow, Emily Austin and an only son, Charles Austin, who was Adam Austin's ancestor. Charles Austin died, details unknown, left a widow Jane Austin and a newborn baby, Freddy Austin. Freddy died leaving a widow three months' pregnant. The next baby born was Peter Austin, who died leaving a wife Sarah, who died of cancer just a year later, and they left a son, Adam Austin, Natalie's husband. He was still a child himself when Sarah died, and he was put in the care of a foster family. Adam Austin left a widow, Natalie Austin" – Sofia briefly glanced up at Natalie before putting her head back down to the screen in embarrassment – "and two children, twins, Alfie and Daisy, both currently missing."

Natalie listened as Marlene broke her entire married life and almost the entire family history of Adam into short bite-sized chunks, seemingly devoid of any emotion as she spoke.

"Is that everything we have?" Sofia asked Marlene.

"It's all I can give you at the moment. We need to fill in the missing bits; the how, when and where they died. If my instincts are correct, it will lead us to the children, best you don't ask how."

"OK, let Sofia do her thing. Go take some air, fill up your coffee cups, Small Batch this time, yes? Come back in say twenty minutes; now go, go." Sofia's fingers started to trace the Austin family tree through the internet before the ladies had even left, her fingers and eyes working together like well-oiled machines.

Natalie looked at her watch.

"You have twenty minutes, at most, and then I'm calling the police; twenty minutes, that's it."

"Come on," Marlene said, taking Natalie's hand. "Let's get that coffee. We'll just be in the way here; Sofia needs her space."

Just fifteen minutes later, five minutes sooner than promised, Sofia's high-pitched voice cut through the noise of the coffee shop. "Darlings, come, come."

She turned back and headed to her office next door. Natalie took a deep breath.

CHAPTER TWENTY-EIGHT

Jesse

J esse stood outside the entrance to the Queens Hotel. It was mid-morning already and the sun was starting to break through the clouds. He turned back to face the sea. It looked beautifully flat and calm, and as ever, he felt it calling him. Any sea swimmer looking over the sea on such a beautiful morning would feel nature calling them and Jesse was no different. He longed to walk across the road right there and then, and dive straight in, washing away all his problems and fears. But he knew he couldn't – not this morning, not now. He looked down and realised he was clutching the diary so tightly that the ends of his fingers were starting to go white. He knew the importance of this moment, for Natalie, for him, for the children, and it would start with the next step he took, but his feet seemed rooted to the spot. The diary had drawn him here to the Queens Hotel and he could feel it starting to burn his fingers, willing him inside. But standing there looking at the entrance, he was frightened. The last time he had seen Lilly he was here and he had almost drowned. That had scared him more than he had admitted to Marlene at the time. But something had changed inside him since his brief flashback to the family car. For the first time in nearly forty years, Jesse had what he'd longed for; a personal connection to his father. And now, he could feel his dad's fear for him and it was holding him back.

He knew he couldn't let the fear take hold, his or his dad's.

"I've got to do it, Dad," he spoke into the morning air, catching the attention of an old couple walking past who assumed he was just another freak talking to an airless mobile phone. "Natalie and Adam need me to do this, I'm the only chance their children have now," he continued, oblivious of the stares from others walking past.

Taking a deep breath, he forced his right foot off the ground and took a step forward. Within just a few steps, he was walking into the Queens Hotel. As he walked in through the door, the air outside the hotel turned bitterly cold, the sky became night dark and the rain started to lash the pavement below. The sign above the hotel door flickered as the wind caught the naked flame of the gas light, casting a shadow down the seafront, its light telling anyone silly enough to be out in such a storm that the Austin Hotel was a place of sanctuary and warmth.

Jesse walked into the lobby, not noticing that the décor was more opulent than it should have been or that the people crowded inside were dressed finely; and some were soaking wet from the evening storm. He did, however, know exactly where he needed to go.

The room he walked into contained a shocking scene. John Austin was lying on the floor, blood pooling around him, and Mary was leaning over him sobbing. Jesse watched as Mary slowly stood up and he saw the realisation on her face that she could do nothing more to save her husband. He watched as she placed her bloodied hands on her stomach and spoke with a fierceness into the silence of the room.

"You will pay for this, Lilly Baker, I swear on all that is holy, you will pay for this forever."

She spun around looking for something. Spotting a lady's hooded cloak on the food counter at the back of the room, she grabbed it, throwing it over her head, covering her body and face completely, and ran back through the room, straight past Jesse, and headed out the door.

This time Jesse did not follow. He turned back to face John Austin lying on the floor as the life drifted away from him. He was still alive, but only barely. He turned his head towards Jesse. He realised that John could see him, and his eyes were calling him over. Jesse knelt next to him, his knees resting in the blood, the thickness of it staining his trousers a dark red and the smell of death causing his throat to contract.

They stared at each other intently.

"Stop her," he croaked. "You have to stop her."

His voice was so low and gurgling from the blood coming from his mouth that Jesse had to lean in close to catch the words.

"You can see me," Jesse said, unable to focus on anything other than the fact that John had spoken to him.

"I shouldn't have done it to her, it's all my fault. Stop her, save us both, please."

John's eyes lost their sparkle as his head rested back into the blood, the life gone from him. Jesse's head swam, he felt sick and he couldn't breathe. He stumbled backwards, slipping in the blood. It was too much, how could John have seen him, spoken to him? Jesse's gift, his curse, was growing too quickly and the power of it was too much for him to control.

Finally, mentally and physically exhausted, he collapsed in the pool of blood next to John Austin.

CHAPTER TWENTY-NINE

Natalie

Marlene led Natalie back next door to Sofia's house. They found her in the front office seated at the table. She had pulled a hidden screen down on the far wall and had attached a small projector to her computer.

"It's was not-so-ard," Sofia started straight in before Natalie and Marlene even had time to find a chair, her high-pitched Spanish accent filling the room as a line of names fell onto the screen in front of them.

John Austin
Harry Austin
Charles Austin
Frederick Austin
Peter Austin
Adam Austin
Daisy Austin
Alfie Austin

Marlene and Natalie read down the list. Natalie caught her breath when she saw Adam's and the twins' names listed. All of them, apart from the twins, long dead. Marlene placed a hand on Natalie's shoulder to comfort her as Sofia carried on talking, unable to see or sense the effect this was having on Natalie.

"This much we already knew; it was all listed on the paper you gave me. I'm not normally so lucky to have papers like these, so much helpful. So I was able to look into local histories. The Austin family have been in Brighton for centuries, much easy for me to find them. Next, I was able to add in the exact dates they all died."

She hit another button on her computer and the list on the screen changed.

John 29/09/1864
Harry 18/09/1911
Charles 24/04/1934
Frederick 18/07/1971
Peter 04/10/1995
Adam 16/8/2016
Daisy
Alfie

"And finally," she said, pressing the button once more, "we can see how they died."

John Austin – Murdered. Stabbed in neck. Murderer never identified. Suspect employee at hotel, unnamed.
Harry Austin – Suspected suicide, clothes found at beach, body not found.
Charles Austin – Drowned in sea. Unexplained.
Frederick Austin – Fall from platform off fishing pier. Fell into sea and drowned, body not found.
Peter Austin – Accidental death. Drowned in accident as fishing boat pushed into pier and sunk. No survivors, no bodies found.
Adam Austin – Suspected suicide. Drowned swimming out into storm, body not found.

Daisy Austin – missing, presumed alive.
Alfie Austin – missing, presumed alive.

"As you can see, the Austin family have saved a lot of money on coffins, ha," Sofia said, before quickly continuing. "So, there is a pattern now; no bodies ever found, and all by or in the ocean from Brighton Beach, blah blah blah. And finally, all men."

"Time's up," Natalie said, having seen over an hour had gone by. "This has been a complete waste of time. I should have called the police, not come here. You should never have made me do this." She turned angrily on Marlene.

"Natalie, please, just wait another minute, just a minute. Sofia, please, your conclusion."

Natalie remained standing, fighting her basic instinct to turn and leave.

"The pattern is clear, I think. All the men in the Austin family going back to John Austin in 1864 have all tragically died. Each one, apart from John Austin, dies in the sea and their bodies not found. And each one left behind a son, who all died in similar circumstances. The date of the first death, John Austin, also coincided with the mysterious death of a lady on the pier, we are assuming this is Lilly Baker and we are assuming her death was linked to the murder of John Austin. So, if we are to believe in ghosts or curses, blah blah blah, and if we believe that somehow Lilly Baker is taking revenge on John Austin, then this would still be happening until something on the pattern changed, which it did."

"They had a girl, Natalie and Adam had twins and *one was a girl*," Marlene chipped in.

"Exactly," Sofia said in triumph, turning to Natalie. "Until now, only boys. Now, you have twins and one is a girl. It has changed, yes. By you having twins, one a girl, you break the curse. Ha, see, all OK now, the curse is broken by the girl, ha."

Natalie turned to Marlene, her face about to explode in anger. "All OK now?" she said, repeating the words in the same high octane Spanish voice of Sofia. "I think it's time we left. My children are missing and I haven't even called the police. We need to go and call them, now." Natalie stood up and waited for Marlene to join her.

"Wait a minute, Natalie. Think about what Sofia just told us. If this is Lilly, and yes she is a curse to the Austins, then we have a link, don't we? Jesse told us that Lilly was pregnant when she died, so she never got to see her baby born. So now she comes back at each new generation and makes sure the same thing happens to John Austin's family. Each of them a father, each of them drowned and their sons doomed to follow. But then you and Adam change things, you have twins, and one of them is a girl, Daisy. All of a sudden, rather than wait for your son to grow up and father a child himself and then kill him, Lilly comes back now. You having twins, one of them a girl, changed things for Lilly."

Natalie locked her eyes onto Marlene's. "But why?" she pleaded, with tears in her eyes. "And why has she taken them? And where are they?" Natalie started to break down in tears of frustration.

"I don't know," Marlene confessed. "That much I don't know." The frustration in Marlene's voice was palpable.

"Maybe she doesn't want to kill your daughter?" Sofia said.

Natalie turned on her. "What then, what the fuck does she want?"

"Her daughter," Marlene said, suddenly understanding where Sofia was going with this.

"Ah ha," Sofia squealed at her friend.

"For Christ's sake, will one of you speak plain English?" Natalie screamed at them.

"Sofia's right," Marlene took over. "Daisy changed everything. Lilly blames the Austins not just for her own death, but for the death of her unborn child as well. Her unborn daughter. She wants Daisy as her own. It's Daisy she wants. Alfie is stuck in the middle of them. She's come back for her daughter."

"Her daughter?" Natalie was still shouting. "Lilly sees Daisy as her unborn daughter?"

"And the pattern?" Sofia prompted her. "The sea?"

"Oh my God, that's it." She grabbed Natalie by the wrist and started pulling her out of Sofia's house. "Call the police, Natalie. Call the police now and get them to the beach."

CHAPTER THIRTY

Jesse

J esse had no idea where he was. He could feel something cold on his forehead and there was a light trying to break into the darkness behind his eyes. He tried to open them, but the light was so strong, it forced them closed again. Faintly, in the distance, a voice called to him. He tried to concentrate on the sounds, but he couldn't make it out. Something cool and wet stroked over his brow, and there was a hand on his wrist.

"Take it easy, buddy," a male voice said as Jesse tried to force his eyes open. "Easy, mate, that's it, slowly does it. Everyone back, please, give us a bit of room."

Jesse's eyes cracked open and he could see the smiling face of a paramedic staring down at him.

"What's your name, my friend?" the man said as he continued to take Jesse's pulse, first at the wrist and then at the neck.

"Err, Jesse."

"Err, Jesse, who? You have a second name, feller?" the paramedic asked.

"Err, of course, Daniels, Jesse Daniels."

"Well, I think you had a bit of a fall, Jesse Daniels. I suspect you'll have a bit of a headache and a bump. Is anything else hurting? Can you move your toes for me, and can you turn your head from side to side? Easy, mate, easy," he said as Jesse started to push himself up on his elbows. "Take it easy, I need to check your neck and your head before you start to move. Hey, Julie," he called to his partner who was across the room talking to the restaurant manager about what he saw. "Come and give me a hand here, will you, before Mr Daniels does himself some permanent harm?"

Julie pounded across the room with all the enthusiasm and speed of the eager twenty-two-year-old she was on her first shout of the day.

"I'm fine, it's all good," Jesse said as he pulled himself up off the floor, just in time for Julie to grab onto him as the dizziness hit him and he stumbled.

"There you go, mate," the paramedic said as he and Julie helped Jesse to a couch nearby. As soon as he'd been sat down, Jesse quickly sprang up again. The two paramedics had no chance against the superior strength of a sea swimmer and were forced back.

"Come on, Jesse, work with us. You need to let us do our jobs, mate," the paramedic said as they tried to ease Jesse back onto the couch.

"The blood," Jesse said, looking around him. "It was everywhere. The couch, the floor. Where's John's body?"

"Go grab Mr Daniels some water, Julie, love. Jesse, mate, you had a fall, OK; we need to work out why for sure, but right now let's just settle down. There's a little blood because you banged your head when you fell, but that's all, and whoever John is he must be OK because he's not here, is he? Now, can you tell me what you think happened?"

Jesse had to think for a moment. He remembered coming into the hotel last night, or was it this morning? It had been light when he came in, he thought, but then it seemed dark and stormy. He came into the room – this room.

Then he remembered it, all of it. Including the taste and smell of John Austin's blood souring his mouth and causing him to gag.

"The diary! Adam's diary. Where is it?" he said as he regained control of himself and pushed again at the man just as he tried to give him some water. The glass hit the floor, shattering into pieces and causing the water to spread over the floor.

"Oh, fantastic, thanks," said the paramedic as he stood back, his top covered in water and glass all over his shoes.

"Do you mean this?" Julie said, picking up the leather diary from the coffee table and handing it to Jesse.

He snatched it off her and shot up from the couch.

"Look, I'm really sorry, really I am. But I'm fine, OK, just a little bump. I've got to go. It's important, really. Sorry," he called again as he ran from the room, the paramedic calling after him as he ran.

Jesse dashed through the lobby of the Queens Hotel, pushing past a young couple just about to check in, and ran out into the sunshine on the seafront. He pulled his mobile phone from his back pocket and was dismayed to see a huge crack running down its face where he must have fallen on it. Carefully, he pressed the round button at the bottom of the screen and was relieved to see the home screen light up. Before he had a chance to search for Marlene's number, the phone rang.

"Marlene!" he shouted into the phone as the wind on the seafront started to pick up and made talking into a phone almost impossible.

"Where are you, Jesse?"

"Outside the Queens Hotel. Where are you two?"

"In the Lanes. We went to see Sofia. She found a link, Jesse. Something that ties up all the deaths. It was Lilly, all of them were."

"Good one, Sherlock," Jesse said sarcastically. "I think we already knew that."

"OK," she said, her tone exasperated. "Just listen, will you? None of the bodies were found, and all were by or in the sea. They never found the bodies because somehow Lilly took them into the sea with her. It would have kept happening if Adam hadn't had a girl and maybe if Adam hadn't reached out to you, Lilly would have taken her by now. It's Daisy she wants. She wants the girl for herself, I don't know why, to take her back with her, maybe, I'm not sure, but Daisy is the key to all this."

It hit Jesse full on. He understood it all.

"She was pregnant, wasn't she? When she fell into the sea she was three months pregnant. She's going to kill Alfie, and she wants Daisy for herself. I get it now. Fuck, why didn't I see it before? There was something about Daisy that was familiar, from the dream and then when I met her. It was like there was something else she was hiding away from me. She's connected to Lilly in every sense, it's as if they are one person, one soul. She's going to kill Alfie and take over Daisy. She's not taking Daisy; she's being reborn into Daisy!" he shouted back to Marlene. "Adam knew as well; he knew he had to somehow stop Lilly from coming back. It was why he pulled me into this. It's why the dreams started and why he drew me into the swimming club. He knew I was the only one who could stop her."

Jesse felt the wind move him across the road and he sensed the light dim slightly as storm clouds appeared across the sky.

"It's happening now," Jesse shouted down the phone. "She's doing it now!"

"If she follows the pattern, she'll take them into the sea by the pier. They're at the beach somewhere, Jesse, get to the beach!" Marlene shouted into the phone, as static took over, making her voice indistinct.

The phone signal failed before Jesse could hear Marlene's final word. But he had understood enough to know that it was now or never. He'd known all along where it would end; deep down, he'd always known that it would end where it had started – on the pier.

He forced his phone back into his jeans pocket and sprinted across the road, narrowly missing the busy traffic. The storm was starting to turn people away from the pier and he found himself having to push his way through a crowd before he could make it to the entrance. She would be here somewhere, he was certain of that, but where?

He ran down the pier, choosing the left side rather than the right, fearing he was going down the wrong part, but equally praying he would see Lilly ahead of him, a child either side of her. The pier was still busy with students and holidaymakers, some hiding under the centre covers, others leaning over the side enjoying watching the seagulls as they hovered in the wind waiting for a child with a bag of fresh doughnuts to walk by. Jesse tried to look at them all in case Lilly was somehow hidden amongst them, going against his instincts that she would likely be under the pier rather than on top of it. He got to the end with its multitude of fairground rides and was hit by the noise as they spun and twisted and threw out lights and loud music in equal intensity. He stopped in the middle of the crowds and turned around, looking intently at everyone and everything; the noises of the people and the rides made it hard for him to concentrate. His phone rattled again in his back pocket. He yanked it out and saw Marlene's number flashing up at him.

"Where are you?" she screamed.

"On the pier."

"I can't hear you, Jesse. Where are you?"

He looked around for a quiet area; there was none. He saw a gap at the end of the pier, in between the carousel and the turbo coaster, and made a run for it, holding the phone to his ear as he ran.

"Wait a minute!" he shouted to Marlene. "Can you hear me now?" he screamed into the phone.

"Where are you?"

"At the end of the pier. Where are you two?"

"We're on our way to you now. She's going to be there, Jesse, I know she is. And she'll have the children with her, you've got to stop her. Natalie's called the police, she told them the children were abducted by a stranger and she thinks they've been taken to the beach. I'm not sure they believed her, but they told her to meet them on the beach by the east of the pier, near your club."

"Marlene, it's too noisy here, I can hardly hear you. Marlene, are you there? Marlene?" Jesse screamed again into the phone.

"Yes," Marlene said, her voice no longer shouting.

"Marlene, what's wrong?" Jesse said, having picked up the change in her tone.

"I don't think she'll be on the pier, Jesse."

"What? What do you mean? I know she's here somewhere. It's always been the pier. It's where she was murdered, you said so yourself."

"She died on the Chain Pier, Jesse, not the Palace Pier – the Palace Pier wasn't even built then."

It hit him like a thunderbolt. Of course. He dropped the phone without realising and ran to the far left of the pier and right to the end, leaning out as far as he could.

CHAPTER THIRTY-ONE

Jesse

From the platform on the Palace Pier, Jesse looked east to where the Chain Pier had been. Up until now, he had always pictured Lilly in his mind by the Palace Pier, under the platform where he stood now, alone in her rowing boat, or teasing John Austin as he swam under the stanchions by the silver ball; but of course, the stanchions were not there back then, none of this was. The Palace Pier stood proudly off the beach while the Chain Pier was almost totally forgotten. But not by Lilly. For at every low tide, especially with the tides that went down to under half a metre, the feet of the old Chain Pier marked the seabed. It was these that had Jesse's attention now.

The tide was currently at its lowest, under a third of a metre, which meant that for the first few hundred metres from the end of the beach it was a slow and cold walk into the sea before you reached swimming depth. And if Marlene was correct, and judging by the storm building up overhead and the way the sea was tearing along from west to east, it was coming in quickly to a very high tide. A dangerous and frightening high tide.

Jesse fixed his eyes on the footprints of the old Chain Pier and watched as they were slowly eaten up by the incoming tide. His eyes followed the line from the beach and he traced them slowly into the sea and out. On a hot summer day and with such a low tide, the sea would usually have been a maelstrom of people –

families, students, visitors and possibly even his swimming club, enjoying a day on Brighton's pebbly beach. But today, with the water temperature only just above twelve degrees, a storm blowing in and a huge tidal surge, the sea was completely empty and the beach had only half a dozen people walking over it.

"You're here somewhere, Lilly, I can feel you," Jesse said to the empty sea as he stared at it. "Come on, come on, show yourself."

She appeared as if from nowhere. Standing at the edge of the beach, her bare feet on the sand as the sea snapped at her ankles. A child stood on either side of her holding onto her hands. Even at that distance, Jesse could see Daisy holding Lilly's left hand and Alfie her right. There was a look of complete calm on both their faces; it caused a shiver to run down his spine.

Jesse watched, transfixed, as Lilly took the first step forward and the children followed willingly.

"No!" he screamed at the top of his voice. "Lilly, no!"

People around him on the end of the pier turned as his screams filled their ears. Some of them kept looking at Jesse, while other followed his eyes out to the sea.

"What's she doing with those children?" one said.

"Oh my God, what's she doing?" another exclaimed.

Jesse turned to them quickly. "You see her?"

"Of course," came the reply. "Who is she? What's she doing?"

Jesse turned back. "Lilly don't do it, Lilly, please, they're just kids, for Christ's sake."

But she didn't look around. They were too far away to hear him. Even if she had wanted to reply, he knew she couldn't.

"Do something!" one of the strangers said, grabbing Jesse by the arm. "They're going to drown."

A crowd had started to gather around Jesse and other people were shouting to the lady in the sea as she slowly kept walking forward, the sea now up to her knees and up to the children's waists.

Jesse could hear the crowd around him going frantic and he

could sense some people running back down the pier to get onto the beach, but he knew that would be no good. They were at least seven hundred metres from the seafront and then another couple of hundred metres down to the beach; even with the energy and legs of an Olympic runner, it would be too far to go before Lilly and the children were completely submerged.

There were people all around him now, some on their phones calling the police while others were calling the seafront office from the emergency number that was hung at the end of the pier. He knew there was only one way he could reach them in time. He pulled his T-shirt over his head, kicked off his shoes and clambered up onto the railings.

"Oi, you! Get down. What are you doing?"

As he climbed up onto the railings, Jesse heard the voice of a security guard who had been sent by the pier management to check why there was a crowd at the end of their pier.

The guard got to the rail, reaching out to grab Jesse back. He got there a fraction of a second too late. Jesse jumped feet first from the end of the pier. He had seen children jumping off the side of the pier hundreds of times in the past, he had even done it himself as a young boy, and he knew how dangerous it was and why the pier management were always on their guard to stop people doing it. He had never jumped from the end, though; he doubted anyone had. It was a long way down and he knew that directly below him, hidden under the water, right at the point where he jumped, was a line of large rocks with metal rings pointing out from their tops where in the old days fishing boats used to moor up before heading up a platform onto the pier. In a high tide, the rings were totally invisible and sat a good two metres below the surface, but in a low tide like today they rested dangerously close to the surface.

Jesse plunged, feet first, and sank under the surface as people up on the pier held their breaths. He felt his right foot brushing against the side of one of the boulders and his left ankle scraped against the other, causing a gash and letting his blood mix with ocean. A few hundred metres away, Lilly felt his pain and picked up her pace. With all his strength, Jesse pulled his knees up into a ball and placed both his feet on the top of one of the rocks and pushed himself up. He broke the surface and grabbed a lungful of air to the relief of the people above him.

Bringing his legs up high, forcing his head and shoulders down into the cold water, he put himself into the natural swimming pose that he had adopted most of his life. His jeans dragged the water and tried to slow him down, but he knew he had so little time and had to plough every inch of strength he had left into getting across the sea to Lilly.

The huge tide coming in meant he was being pushed east towards them at a rapid pace, and the prevailing winds coming from the west pushed him even further; still, he knew he was a long way off and he could picture Lilly and the children getting deeper and deeper until he couldn't see them anymore.

He dug as deep as he could and forced his way through the waves as the wind started to chop up the sea. In his head, he kept repeating to himself, *it's just a swim, one arm over the other, reach, stretch, pull*. He knew the danger he was in if he lost his composure. He needed speed, as much as he could create, but if he pushed it too hard and went hell for leather, he would lose his stroke and end up bullying his way through the water rather than gliding through it as he had to. He needed to stay calm, keep his body up high, his chin and shoulders down low and his stroke rate steady; one arm over the other – reach, stretch and pull; reach, stretch and pull.

But also, he needed to see where he was going. The sea was tossing him all over the place and it was all he could do to maintain his position and stroke rate, but if he didn't break form and take a look, he could find himself well past them and unable to swim back against the incoming tide. He slowed his arms down to half speed and thrust his head up to the surface just as a wave hit him from the side, causing him to take down a lungful of salt water and spinning him off his natural axis. He coughed out the water and forced himself to a complete stop just as another wave washed over him, pushing his head back into the sea. He dragged his legs down under him, pushed himself up high out of the water and spun towards where he hoped Lilly would be.

She was still there, almost in front of him, just a couple of metres away. The sea had pushed him quickly, moving him at over four miles an hour, but if he didn't change direction soon, the tide would send him right past her and he knew he wouldn't have the strength to swim back against it. In his quick glance, he could see the water was almost up to the twins' shoulders and just past Lilly's chest; a few seconds more and they would be taken under. Jesse forced himself back into his swim position and reached his right arm out once more, pulling himself at a steep angle back to shore, covering the last two metres like a rocket.

He dropped his feet right in front of them, finding the flat sandy seabed and standing up straight, the water up high around his chest. A rolling wave crashed into his back and pushed him forward into Lilly. He put his hands out to stop himself, but they went straight through her and he had to plant his feet firmly down to stop himself falling. He pulled himself up again and turned to them, praying for a break in the waves. Lilly and the children stopped walking and she looked up at Jesse.

She didn't speak, but he heard her, nonetheless. "You're too late," her voiced whispered into his head.

Lilly's face was impassive, not a movement, not even a blink from her eyes, just the smallest smile on her pale lips, barely perceptible.

Jesse reached out and tried to grab Alfie but his hand touched nothing. "What have you done to them?" he shouted.

Lilly took a step forward with Alfie and Daisy, causing Jesse to step back into the waves.

"No, I won't let you!" he roared.

From behind him, a wave curled past, missing him, but crashing into Lilly and the children, making them stumble back a few more steps. Lilly howled into the sky as the wave hit her.

"The waves, they hurt you, the waves that killed you still hurt you!" he screamed through the wind. Lilly's sudden pain brought Alfie and Daisy out of her spell.

"Where am I?" Alfie screamed, trying to pull free of Lilly and falling back under the surface. Jesse leapt forward and grabbed him before the sea took him under. He could hold him now; Alfie was here in the flesh. He tried to pull him close, but Daisy had reached out for her brother, grabbed his arm fiercely and pulled him back to her and Lilly.

"Daisy, don't!" Alfie screamed, but Daisy held on tight as Lilly forged forward again through the waves.

The waves had now forced Jesse behind them, with his back to the beach. They turned to face him, keeping their own backs to the waves; all of them now facing each other, Jesse and Lilly eye to eye. Jesse heard voices shouting from the beach. He half turned, scared to break the spell he had over Lilly.

A coastguard and a policeman were wading out to them, Marlene and Natalie only a few steps behind. All of them forcing their way through the incoming tide and oblivious to the cold water biting through their clothes and the danger that they were all now in.

"Let the children go!" the policeman shouted across the sea, Natalie and Marlene adding their voices to the swirl around them.

Jesse turned back to Lilly.

"Let them go, Lilly, don't do it," Jesse pleaded with her.

Jesse caught a glimpse of Alfie's terrified face, tears streaming down his cheeks, as Lilly pulled him and Daisy under the waves with her. Jesse rushed forward to the spot where they went under and dived down. He frantically looked around, searching with his hands and his eyes, the sea salt stinging his pupils as he spun in circles under the waves.

He couldn't find them; they had gone.

He dived down again, just as one of the coastguards caught up and went under next to him. Marlene and Natalie reached the spot together as the coastguard sprang up, drawing in as much air as she could to fill her aching lungs. She stood there, with Natalie and Marlene, scanning the sea as the waves forced them back to the shore.

"There!" Marlene screamed as she saw movement twenty metres in front of them.

"There."

Jesse surfaced, half-drowned from being under so long; a child was in his arms, just one child.

He stumbled forward, crashing into Natalie as she caught him. She pulled Daisy from his arms into her own and squeezed her so tightly she could hardly breathe as the water expelled from her lungs. Marlene heaved Jesse up as he too sank beneath the waves with exhaustion.

The coastguard, having dived under again, came up to the surface and grabbed a lungful of air before plunging back under again. It was only seconds before she would be able to wade back to shore, the sea now up to her chin, her own search for the boy over.

The policeman who had just arrived on the scene helped Natalie as she came out of the sea and back onto the beach, carrying Daisy in her own arms, where others waited for them. Marlene reached out to help Jesse, but he wasn't willing to let Lilly take Alfie in the same way she had taken all the Austin men before him. He pulled away from her and dived back under.

"Jesse, it's too late!" Marlene shouted, but he was already gone before the words reached him.

Back on the beach, a crowd had gathered, along with more police and volunteers from the seafront office. As her colleagues led her away, a blanket over her shoulders, the female coastguard looked back to Natalie wanting to say how sorry she was that she couldn't save her son, but she had no words, all she had were tears that mingled with the salty sea dripping down from her sodden hair.

Natalie wrapped herself around Daisy, unable to comprehend what she had witnessed, and what else she may have lost.

Another member of the coastguard team waded out into the sea and managed to reach Marlene before the waves dragged her under as well.

"Please, you've got to come with me!" he shouted to Marlene above the wind.

"... but Jesse," she responded weakly, the cold starting to affect her speech.

"It's too late, we need to get back," he insisted.

Marlene was by now too cold and weak to resist and allowed him to drag her back to the shore. She stumbled onto the beach as wave after wave hit her from behind, each one sapping her energy further. The coastguard managed to get her onto the beach next to Natalie as he ran off to find a blanket.

"Alfie..." Natalie pleaded with her. But Marlene had no words left.

"There, look, he's got him." A voice from the crowd drew everyone's attention back to the sea.

Jesse was standing, the sea breaking over his head. The young child was in his arms; he held him high above the waves as he fought his way back to shore. The young coastguard spun around, ran back to the sea and dived in, swimming as hard as he could until Jesse and Alfie were right by him.

"Take the boy," Jesse said weakly. The coastguard did as Jesse instructed him and took Alfie's lifeless body, holding his head out of the water, as two members of the public rushed into the sea and helped him get Alfie onto the shore.

As the paramedic breathed life back into the young boy, Jesse was helped from the sea by another two volunteers.

With the little strength he had left in him, Jesse pushed his helpers away and stumbled over to Natalie, throwing himself in front of her and grabbing Daisy by her arms, pulling her in face to face.

"Mum!" Daisy screamed.

"Jesse!" Marlene and Natalie shouted together.

Daisy opened her eyes, which were no longer the emerald green she had inherited from her father; they were now shining a bright blue as they stared back into Jesse's.

He fell back onto the stony beach as Natalie grabbed Daisy and pulled her in close. Marlene reached Jesse a slight second after and took him by the shoulders.

"Jesse, it's over, you did it, you saved them both."

"I was too late, she won."

"You saved them, Jesse. Both of them. Look, see, they're safe now."

Jesse watched as the paramedics and the police helped Natalie and her children up the beach to the waiting ambulance.

"I lost her," he sobbed, falling onto the stones.

"What do you mean? Jesse, what do you mean?" Marlene asked him, but he couldn't respond.

He was no longer there. In his mind, he was back in a car with his parents and his own twin sister, singing silly French songs as they headed out on a family holiday.

"Come on, mate, let's get you up to the ambulance as well, you're a bloody hero," the policeman said as he tried unsuccessfully to help Jesse to his feet.

At the ambulance, Natalie sat watching as Alfie was wrapped in a blanket and given oxygen, the life slowly coming back to him.

Daisy, wrapped in a silver foil cloak, sat by her mum and took her hand.

Natalie smiled a smile of relief.

Daisy wrapped her fingers around her mum's. Natalie looked down at her daughter and into the unfamiliar eyes that stared back at her as a sharp perfume seeped into her lungs, causing an itch in her throat.

"It's OK, Mummy, we're together now, just us, one big happy family."

Jesse

J esse had been cycling for most of the morning.

He had cycled over six hundred and fifty miles so far in the two weeks since he had left Brighton.

After leaving the hospital and going back to his flat, he had locked the door, shut the curtains and hidden away. Despite not being a drinker, he still managed to find solace in a bottle of Johnny Walker Black Label, his dad's favourite drink; it was pretty much all he knew about him. Since the last time, he had not been able to contact his dad, or even feel his spirit, and it was yet another loss he had to bear.

He knew he would never be able to come to terms with what happened. In his dreams, he no longer saw Lilly Baker, she was now completely lost to him, but he did sometimes see Daisy. He had tried to reach out to her to start with, to find her hidden deep within, but each time he was blocked, he was no longer welcome there.

After two weeks of locking himself away and avoiding contact with Marlene, he had packed a small bag and headed into Hove to the offices of Mishon Mackay lettings.

"You got another place for me, Jesse?" Alex Mackay asked him when he walked through the door. "I thought I had filled all the flats for you."

"It's my one, on the top floor."

"You moving? I thought you loved it there."

"I just need a break for a while, that's all."

"OK, no problem at all, it'll rent easily. How much and for how long?"

Jesse gave Alex the keys and told him at least a year, maybe more, and the same rent as the others. He gave him an email address where he could contact him and asked him to send any post he might have to his brother's bike shop. Then he left the office, put his rucksack on his back and climbed onto his trusty old touring bike.

Before he left Brighton, he cycled down to the seafront for a last time and then along the two-mile stretch to the Palace Pier, breathing in the sea air. He missed swimming in the sea so much, but for the moment he was too frightened to go back into it. It was still too soon; maybe it would be something that he could never go back to. As well as everything else, it seemed Lilly had also stolen the sea from him.

He started the long ride to the Channel Tunnel at Dover. He was in no rush. The cycle to Dover was an uneventful but draining ninety miles. After arriving in Calais on the Eurostar, he set up his GPS tracker and entered in his final destination – some 670 miles distant. He calculated in his head that if he did about seventy miles a day, even taking into account the hills between Calais and Provence, it should take him about ten days. He could have stayed in hotels along the route, there were plenty available and money was never a problem for him, but he didn't want comfort, or company. Instead, he chose to stop on old farmland or hidden campsites; places where he could hide away in the corner of a field and not engage with anyone.

Today was day ten. He had made good time, even by his standards. His Garmin told him that he would reach his destination by midday.

Since leaving the campsite in the small village of Beaumes-de-

Venise that morning, he had already ridden twenty miles up and over four peaks, the last one reaching a height of over eight hundred metres. He now found himself coasting back down the other side and heading for the village of Malaucene, to the base of Le Mont Ventoux, his final destination. Le Mont Ventoux, also known as the Giant of Provence, was the terror of the Tour de France. It stood 1,912 metres above sea level and was one of cycling's most iconic climbs. It was also the place where Jesse's dad had rolled his car down the side of the mountain, killing himself, his wife and Jesse's twin sister, leaving Jesse an orphan at the age of four.

Jesse reached Malaucene almost exactly at midday; as usual, the Garmin didn't let him down. He dismounted next to the small road sign that read Mt Ventoux and took a deep breath. The last time he had been here he had lost everything. The police report that he had seen when he had been old enough to face it said that it was a tragic family accident; and up until recently, he had no reason to disbelieve it. But during the last session with Marlene when he found himself back in the car, he had felt something else, a sense of fear that should not have been there. He was not sure what it meant, but it had definitely come from his dad. It was a feeling of trying to protect his family and take them somewhere safe – away from something, or someone. But at the time he felt it, he was in the back seat of the car with his sister, and his dad's fear seemingly had nothing to do with an impending car accident; it was something that was already there within his dad.

When he'd left Brighton two weeks before, he'd known exactly where he needed to go; he just didn't know what it was he would find when he got there.

He climbed back onto his bike and started the slow, hard climb up the mountain. A sign showed the first part of the climb would reach an exhausting nine percent gradient and the entire climb to the top would be over twenty kilometres of sheer hard work cycling upwards without flat road at any stage.

He sensed the other cyclists before he saw them. He could feel them behind him getting closer, pulling towards him with every turn of the pedals. The peloton was small, just five of them, but they were fast and they blew past him, knocking him sideways with the wind as they went. He suddenly felt a need to catch them, to no longer be on the Ventoux on his own. He forced his clipped feet back into the pedals and turned his legs as fast as he could. Jesse knew how to cycle fast, he had cycled all his life, and he threw the gears into their lowest and pushed his cadence as hard as he could, forcing his bike on and up at an unnatural speed. He hit the first corner at a gradient of almost six percent and saw the back of the peloton; it spurred him on. He was catching them pedal by pedal. He put his head down, pushed harder and powered up to the next corner, turning into it with all his strength. He was now at their back, almost on the wheel of the rear rider. He kept his eyes down, focusing on the back wheel in front of him as it turned another corner, this one steeper still, starting to reach the nine percent the sign promised. The rest of the peloton was pulling away, but Jesse stuck to the one in front of him at the rear of the group, keeping as close to him as he could, unwilling to let him get away.

Without any warning, the bike reared left, off the main road, and hurtled down a bank. Jesse followed; he had no idea why, but it was as if he were attached to the bike in front by an invisible cord. The cyclist flew right over the edge of the mountain, sailing downwards. Jesse jumped from his bike at the very last second, skidding on his side to the edge. He managed to grab a tree root, almost pulling his wrist out of the socket and jolting himself to a stop on his back, his legs precariously hanging over the side of the mountain. His bike carried on without him and hit the road below, splintering into pieces. But it was the other cyclist that Jesse was focused on. He fell fast and hard, but never reached the bottom. In the split seconds before he was about to crash to his death, the cyclist's head turned and caught Jesse's eyes. Jesse saw a look of pleading in the eyes and felt helplessness and pain wash over him.

A voice screamed into Jesse's head. The shock sent him tumbling back as if he had been punched hard on the nose.

He managed to grab a final look over the edge as he fell backwards and saw the cyclist and bike vanish into thin air. Tentatively, Jesse looked over the side. His bike lay smashed across the road below; but there was nothing else, no other bike, no other cyclist. But he had been there, the other cyclist, they all had, the entire peloton. Jesse has seen them; he had felt them rush past him.

He pulled himself up. His rucksack had protected his back from being torn by the loose stones before it was ripped open, spilling its contents. At that moment, he couldn't have cared less for the clothes and tent now covered in dust and spread over the mountainside.

His arm and shoulder throbbed and blood trickled from the cuts down his legs. But he was oblivious to it all.

All he could think about was the helplessness of the cyclist as he plunged to his death and the voice in his head calling for his help.

Jesse needed to get back down to the village of Malaucene, he needed to know more about who the man was, about anyone who had died on the Ventoux, all thoughts of finding out about his dad's car crash now forgotten. He needed to help the cyclist. Someone else other than his own family had died on the Giant of Provence that day and whoever it was needed the ghost hunter.

Acknowledgements

Mel Whitehouse and Gillian Holmes, whose editing shaped and reshaped my story and who stopped me constantly shooting off in the wrong directions.

My readers, particularly my brother-in-law, Darren Abrahams, who is a constant inspiration to me, and to Geoff Dismorr from my swimming club whose honest critique was a relief.

Thanks to the Faber Academy for showing me I can finish writing a book after all.

Made in the USA
Monee, IL
01 September 2024

65032177R00152